A Decade of Love Songs & Wedding Hits
1990-2000

Project Manager: Carol Cuellar
Book Art Layout: Joe Klucar

Contents

ALL 4 LOVE

Lyric and Music by
COLOR ME BADD and
HOWARD THOMPSON

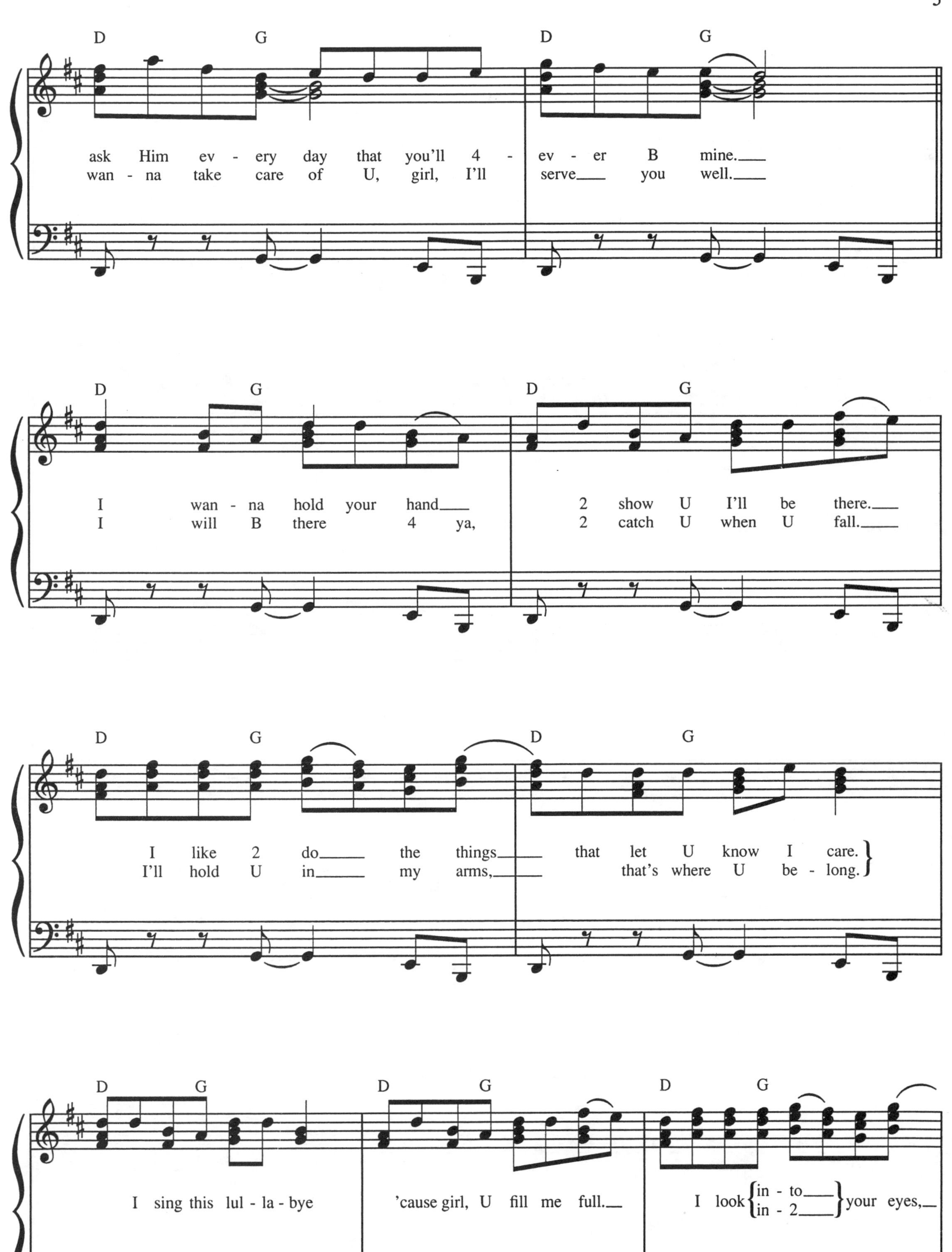
D G D G
ask Him ev - ery day that you'll 4 - ev - er B mine.
wan - na take care of U, girl, I'll serve you well.
D G D G
I wan - na hold your hand 2 show U I'll be there.
I will B there 4 ya, 2 catch U when U fall.
D G D G
I like 2 do the things that let U know I care.
I'll hold U in my arms, that's where U be - long.
D G D G D G
I sing this lul - la - bye 'cause girl, U fill me full. I look in - to / in - 2 your eyes,

1.
To Next Strain
2.
N.C.
D
G
D
G
you're so beau - ti - ful.
you're so beau - ti - ful...
beau - ti - ful...
N.C.
Chorus:
D
G
D
G
yeah!
Oh, girl, I think I love ya.
I'm al - ways think-ing of ya.
D
G
D
G
I want ya to know I do it
all 4 love.
D
G
D
G
I love it when we're to - geth - er.
Girl, I need you 4 - ev - er,
1.
D.S.
2.
To Next Strain
D
G
N.C.
N.C.
and I want U 2 know I do it
all 4 love.
all 4 love.

3. 4. etc.
Repeat ad lib. and fade
N.C.
D G
D G
all___ 4 love.__
all,
Spoken: Yo! Come here, sweetheart.
The distance B-tween us,
all,
I want U 2 know something, alright.
an ocean of tears.

1.
2.
D G
D G
D G
all, all, all, all, all,
See, every day N my life without U would
See, all the things I do 4 U
all.
B like a hundred years.
all.
are 4 love.
Dig it.

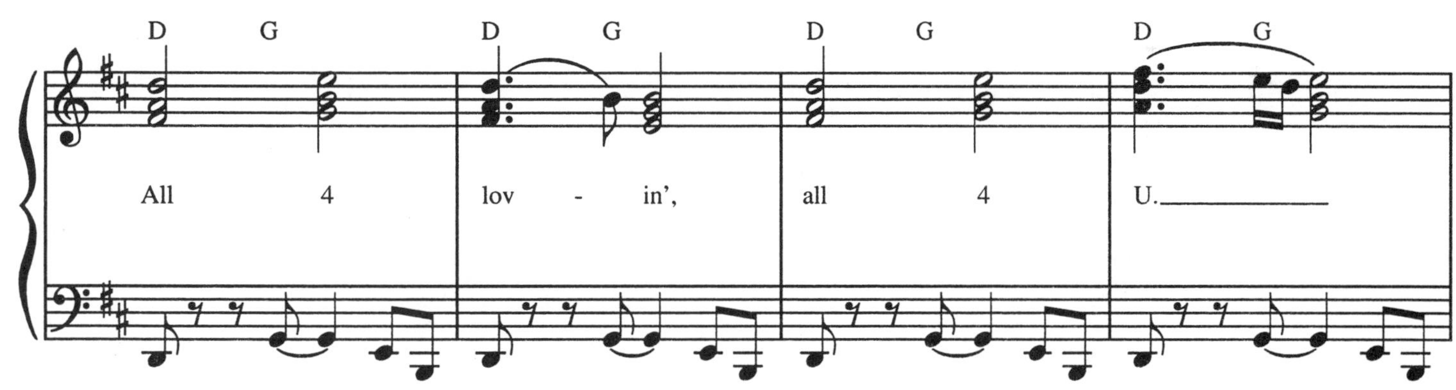
D G
D G
D G
D G
All 4 lov - in', all 4 U.___

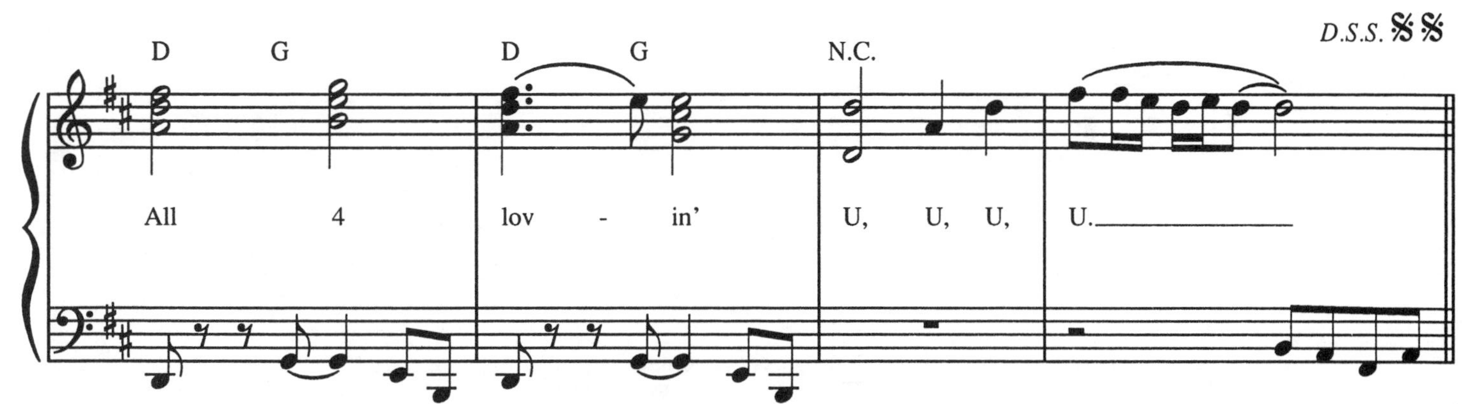
D.S.S.
D G
D G
N.C.
All 4 lov - in' U, U, U, U.___

From the Original Motion Picture Soundtrack "THE THREE MUSKETEERS"

ALL FOR LOVE

Written by
BRYAN ADAMS, ROBERT JOHN "MUTT" LANGE
and MICHAEL KAMEN

Verse:
A
D
Dsus
Rod:
hold. 2. When there's love in - side,
then there's a rea - son why.
Bryan: I swear I'll al - ways be strong.
Rod: then it's love you take.
(3.) Sting: I'll be the fire in your night.
D
D/F♯
G
3
Both: I'll be the world that pro - tects you
I'll prove to you we be - long.
All: I'll be there when you need me
I will de - fend I will fight.
D/A
A
Asus
A
from the wind and the rain, from the hurt and the pain.
when hon - or's at stake, this vow I will make:
cresc.

Chorus:
D Em7 D/F♯ N.C. D/F♯ G
All: Let's make it / that it's all for one, all for love.
mf
Em7 D/A
Let the one you hold be the one you want, the one you
A D/F♯ G Bm A D/F♯ G
need. 'Cause when it's all for one, it's one for all. When there's
Em7 D/F♯ G D/A
some - one that you know, then just let your feel - ings show and make it

1.
D.S. 𝄋
2.
G D/F♯ Em7 A
D
Dsus
D
all for one, all for love.
all,
Bryan: 3. When it's love you make,
dim.
mp
Bridge:
Bm
G
Em7 D/F♯ G A
Don't lay our love to rest, 'cause we could stand up to the test. We've got
Bm
D/F♯
G Asus A
ev - 'ry - thing and more than we had planned, more than the riv -
Bm
D/F♯
G
A
- ers that run the land, we've got it all in our hands.

1.
G
Em7
Dsus
D
(Instrumental solo . . .
Dsus
D
2.
Asus
A
N.C.
. . . end solo)
Now, it's
Chorus:
G
Em7
all for___ one, all for love.___
Let the one you hold be the one you_
D/A
A
D/F♯
G
Bm
A
D/F♯
want, the one you_ need. 'Cause when it's all for___ one, it's one for all.__

G
Em7
D/F♯
When there's some - one that you know, then just
G
D/A
G/B
D/F♯
let your feel - ings show. When there's some - one that you want, when there's
G
D/A
Em
N.C.
some - one that you need, let's make it all, all for one,
slower
a tempo
Gm7
Gm(maj7)
Gm/A
D
D(2)
and all for love.
mp slower
a tempo
rit. e dim.
p

ALL I HAVE TO GIVE

Words and Music by
FULL FORCE
Moderately ♩ = 96
G♭ A♭ B♭m G♭ A♭ Fm G♭
1. I don't know
Verse:
G♭ A♭ B♭m G♭ A♭
what he does to make you cry, but I'll be there to make you smile.
does it seem like he's not e - ven lis-t'ning to a word you say?
Fm G♭ A♭ A♭/C D♭
I don't have a fan - cy car to get to you. I'll
That's O. K., babe, just tell me your prob - lems. I'll try my best to
mf

C♭maj7
Fm7/B♭
B♭m
G♭
A♭
walk a thou - sand miles. I don't care if he buys
kiss them all a - way. Does he leave when you need
B♭m
G♭
A♭
Fm
G♭
you nice things. Do his gifts come from the heart? I don't know,
him the most? Do his friends get all your time? Ba - by, please,
A♭
C♭maj7
B♭m7
but if you were my girl, I'd make it so we'd
I'm on my knees pray - ing for the
Fsus
F
B♭m
nev - er be a - part.
day when you'll be mine.
But my love is all

Chorus:

Gb Ab Bbm Gb Ab

I have to give. Without you, I don't think I can live.

Fm Gb Ab Ab/C Db

I wish I could give the world to you, but love is all I

Cbmaj7 1. Gb/Ab 2. Gb/Ab

have to {give. / give.} 2. When you talk to you.

Bridge:

Db Ab/C Db Gb Ab/C Db

Hey, girl, hey, girl, I don't want you to cry no more inside.

Gb
Ab
Bbm
Ab/C
Db
Gb
All the mon - ey in the world could nev - er
Ab/C
Db
Cbmaj7
Ab/Bb
Bbm
add up to all the love I have in - side. I love you,
Gb
Ab
Bbm
Gb
Ab
ba - by. And I will give it to you.
Bbm
Gb
Ab
Bbm
All I can give, all I can give. All, all, all, all. Ev-'ry-thing I have is for you.

G♭
A♭
Fm
G♭
A♭
You got what you need. You got what I need. My love is
A♭/C
D♭
C♭maj7
A♭sus
all that I have_ to give.___ All that I have_ is for you.___ My love is all__
Chorus:
G♭
A♭
B♭m
G♭
A♭
___ I have__ to give.___ With-out you, I don't___ think I____ can live.__
Fm
G♭
A♭
A♭/C
D♭
___ I wish I could give___ the world_ to you,___ but love is all I

C♭maj7
G♭/A♭
N.C.
have to give. But my love is all I have to give.
Fm
G♭
With-out you, I don't think I can live. I wish I could give
A♭
A♭/C
D♭
C♭maj7
B♭m
the world to you, but love is all I have to give
G♭/A♭
G♭
A♭
B♭m
N.C.
to you. But my love is all

Chorus:
G
A
Bm
G
A
I have to give. With-out you, I don't think I could live.
F♯m
G
A
A/C♯
D
I wish I could give the world to you, but love is all I
Cmaj7
A/G
Repeat ad lib. and fade
have to give. But my love is all

ALL MY LIFE

Words and Music by
RORY BENNETT and
JO JO HAILEY

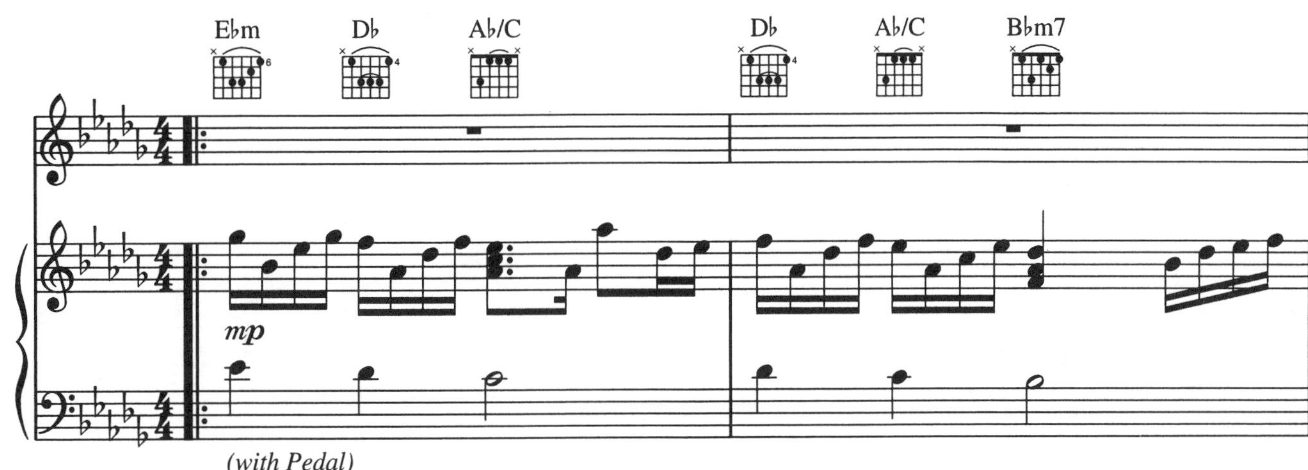

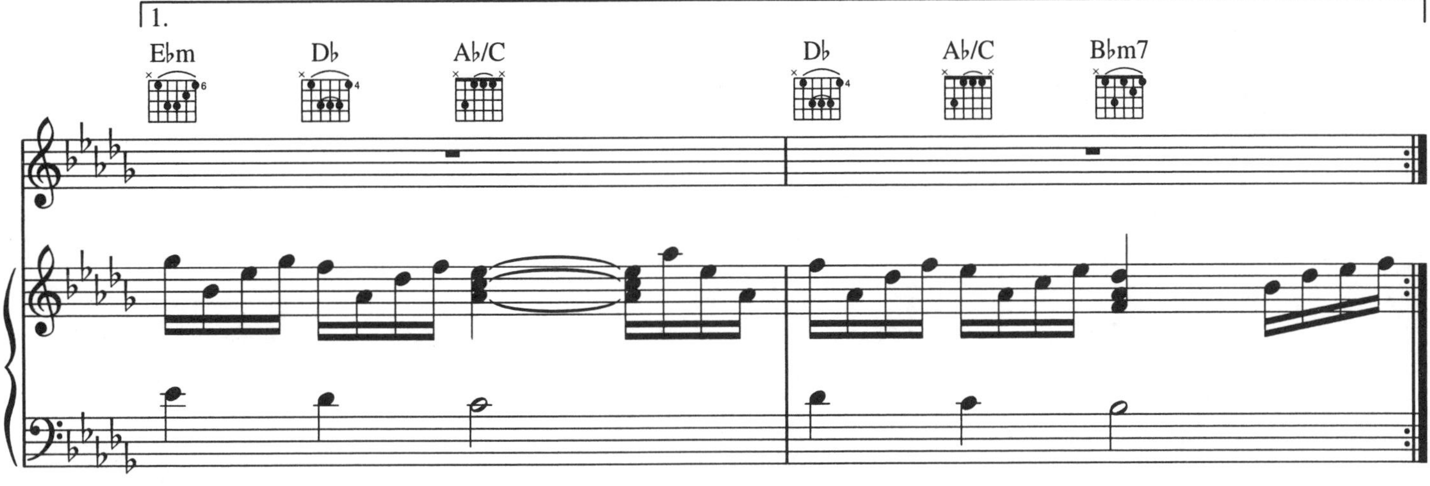

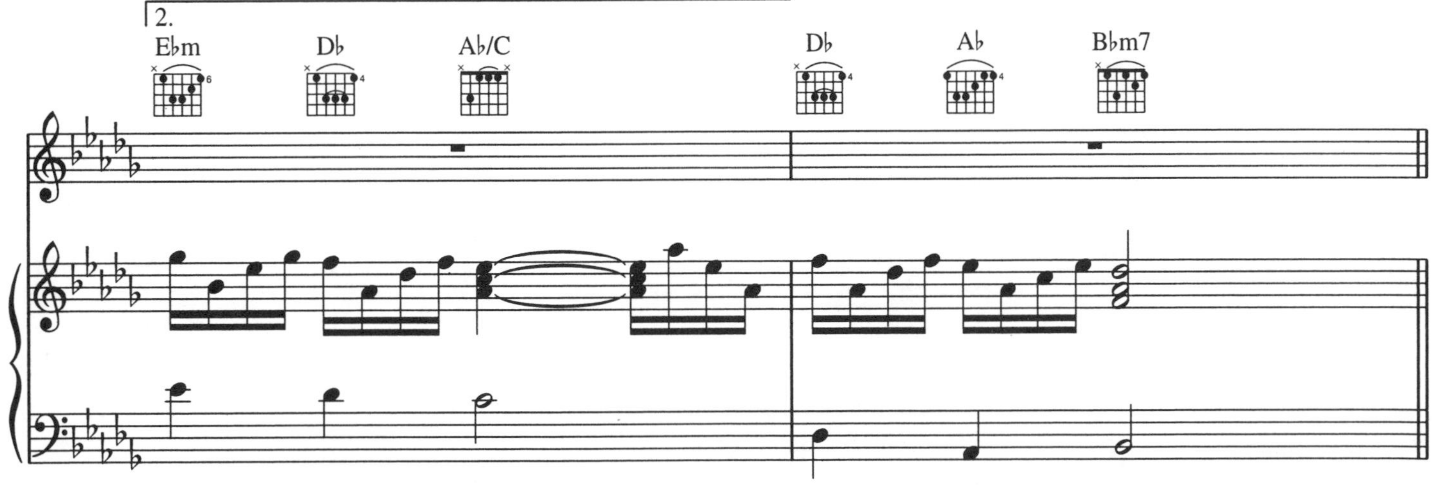

Verse:
Db Ab/C Bbm7 Gb Ab
1. I will nev-er find an-oth-er lov-er sweet-er than you, sweet-er than you.__ And
Db Ab/C Bbm7 Gb Ab
I will nev-er find an-oth-er lov-er more pre-cious than you,__ more pre-cious than you.__ Girl, you are
Db Ab/C Bbm7 Gb Ab
close to me, you're like my moth-er; close to me, you're like my fa-ther; close to me, you're like my sis-ter; close to me, you're like my broth-er.
2. See additional lyrics
Bbm7 Ab Gb Ebm7 Ab Ab/C
You are the on - ly one,__ you're my ev-'ry-thin', and for you this song__ I sing. In

Chorus:
E♭m
D♭
A♭/C
D♭
A♭/C
B♭m7
all my life, I pray for some-one like you. And
E♭m
D♭
A♭/C
D♭
Fm
B♭m7
I thank God that I fi-nal-ly found you.
E♭m
D♭
A♭/C
F/A
F/C
B♭m
A♭
All my life, I pray for some-one like you, and I
G♭
A♭
B♭m
A♭
B♭m
A♭/C
D♭
A♭/C
B♭m
A♭
hope that you feel the same way too. Yes, I

1.
G♭ A♭ B♭m A♭ B♭m A♭/C D♭ B♭m
pray that_ you do love_ me too._____
G♭ A♭ D♭ B♭m
G♭ A♭
2.
G♭ A♭ B♭m A♭ B♭m A♭/C
2. Say, and I pray that_ you do love_ me. You're

Bridge:
Ebm
Ab/C
F
F/A
Bbm
Bb/D
all that I ev - er know; when you smile on my face, all I see is a glow. You turn
my life a - round, you pick me up when I was down. You're
all that I ev - er know; when you smile, my face glow. You pick me up when I was down. Say, you
all that I ev - er know; when you smile, my face glow. You pick me up when I was down. And I
Ab

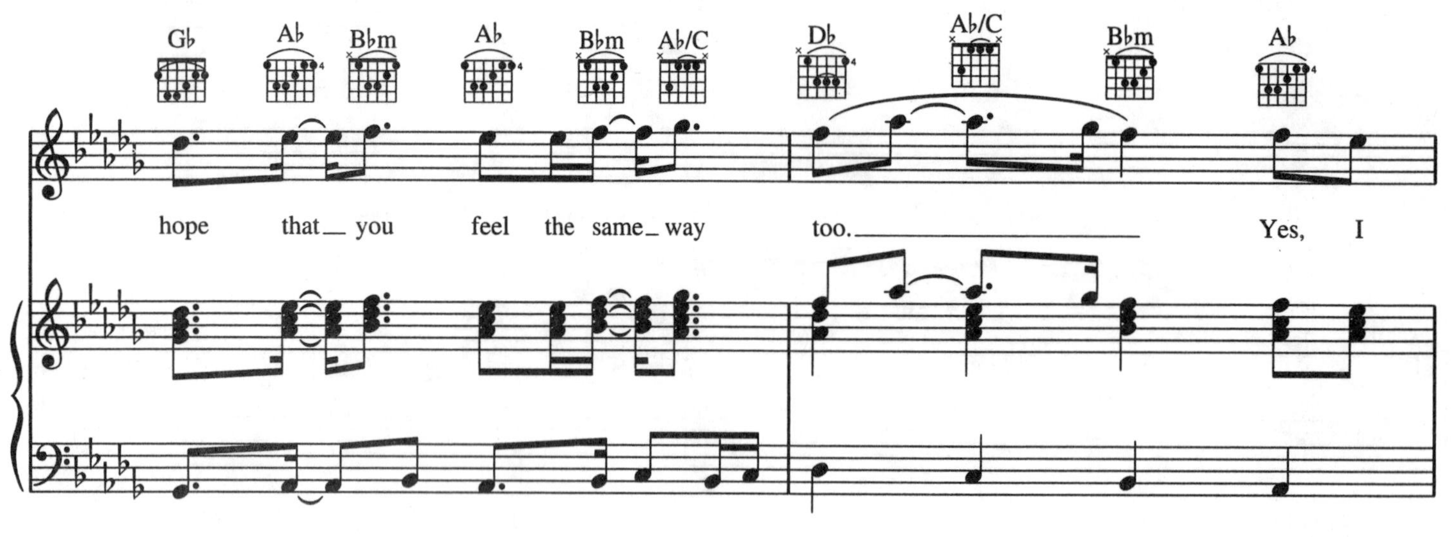
Gb Ab Bbm Ab Bbm Ab/C Db Ab/C Bbm Ab
hope that_ you feel the same_ way too.___ Yes, I

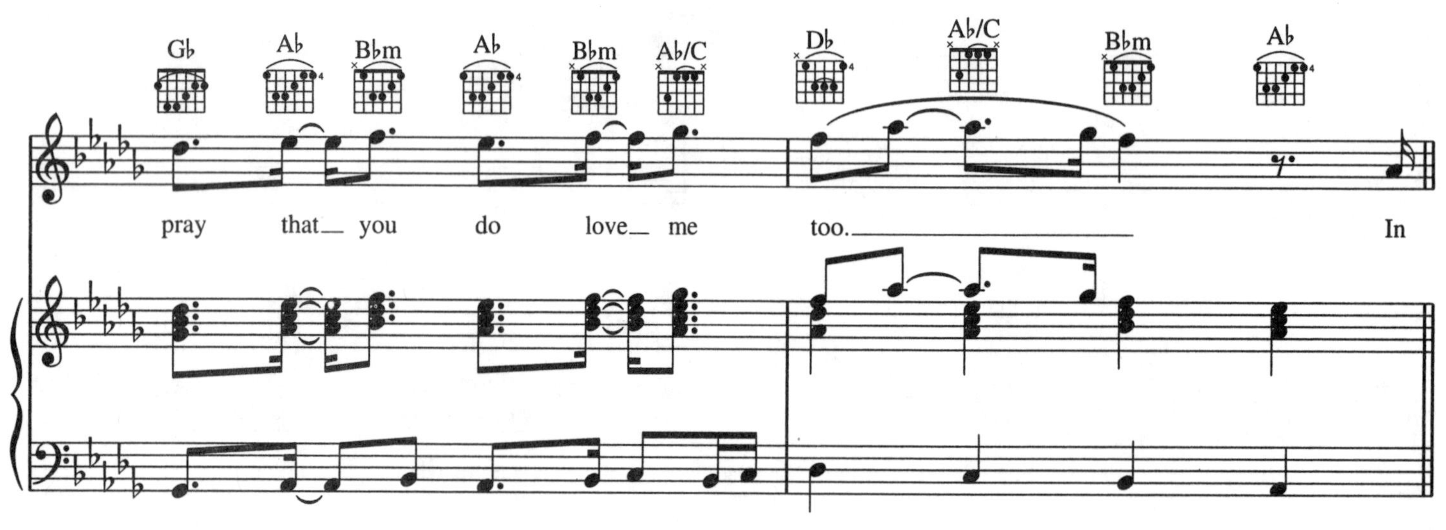
Gb Ab Bbm Ab Bbm Ab/C Db Ab/C Bbm Ab
pray that_ you do love_ me too.___ In

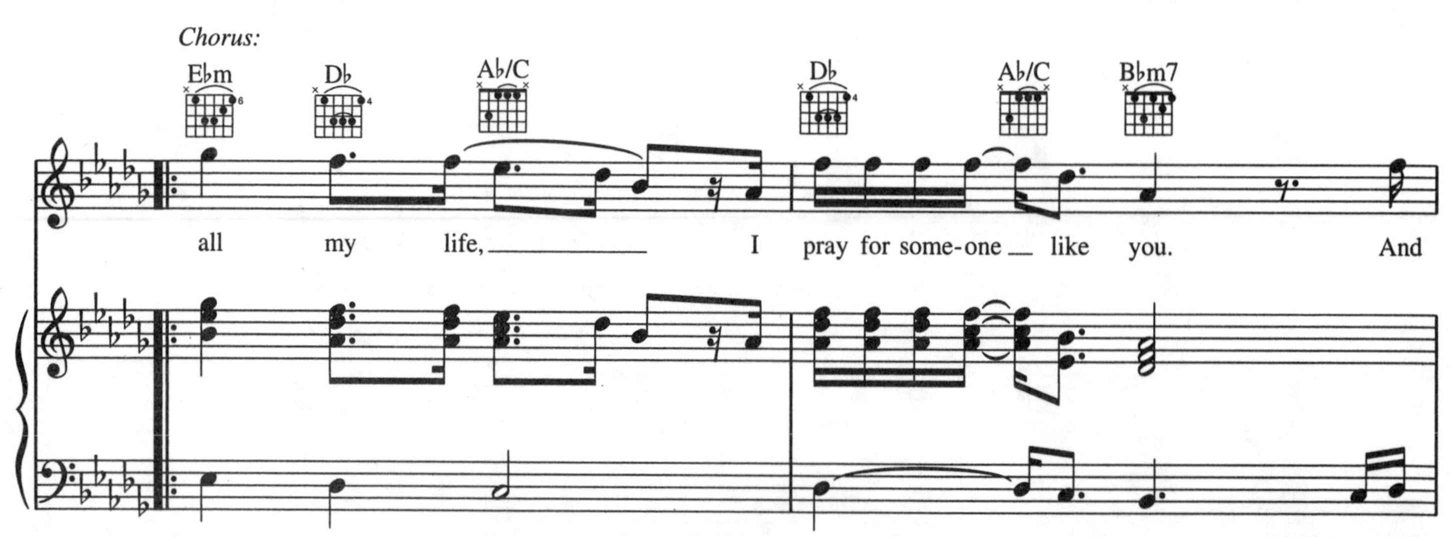
Chorus:
Ebm Db Ab/C Db Ab/C Bbm7
all my life,___ I pray for some-one_ like you. And

Verse 2:
Say, and I promise to never fall in love with a stranger.
You're all I'm thinkin', love, I praise the Lord above
For sendin' me your love, I cherish every hug.
I really love you so much.
(To Chorus:)

ALWAYS AND FOREVER

Words and Music by
ROD TEMPERTON

Slowly ♩. = 50

Emaj9 B/C♯ C♯m7 Amaj9 F♯m7/B

Ooh!

mp

(with pedal)

Emaj9 B/C♯ C♯m7

And I know to-mor-row will still be the same,
And if you get lone-ly, call me and take

Amaj9 Emaj9 F♯m7 F♯m7/B

'cause we've got a life of love that won't ev-er change.
a sec-ond to give to me that mag-ic you make. } And

cresc.

Chorus:

Emaj9 F♯m7 G♯m7 Amaj9 G♯m7 F♯m7

ev - 'ry day love me your own spe - cial way. Melt all my

mf

F♯m7/B Emaj9 G♯m7

heart a - way with a smile.

Amaj9 G♯m7 F♯m7 G♯m7
Take time to tell me you really care and
Amaj9 G♯m7 F♯m7 F♯m7/B Emaj9 G♯m7
we'll share to-mor-row to-geth-er. Ooh ba-by,
1.
Amaj9 G♯m7 F♯m7 F♯m7/B N.C. Emaj9 Em7/A F♯m7/B
I'll al-ways love you for-ev-er. Ev-er, ev-er, ev-er!
(Al-ways for-ev-er love you.)
2.
Amaj9 G♯m7 F♯m7 F♯m7/B N.C. Emaj9
I'll al-ways love you for-ev-er.
(Al-ways for-ev-er love

Em7/A
F♯m7/B
Emaj9
Ooh ba-by, ooh ba - by. Yeah ba-by, yeah ba - by. For-ev - er.
you.)
(Al-ways for - ev - er love
Em7/A
F♯m7/B
Emaj9
Love you! Love you! You! You! Al - ways.
you.)
(Al-ways for - ev - er love
Em7/A
F♯m7/B
Emaj9
Ev - er, ev - er, ev - er! For - ev - er.
you.)
(Al-ways for - ev - er love
Em7/A
F♯m7/B
Emaj9
Al - ways. Oh! Ooh love, love
you.)
(Al-ways for - ev - er love

Em7/A
F♯m7/B
Emaj9
you. Ev - er, ev - er, ev - er!
you.)
And al - ways, I'll love
(Al - ways for - ev - er love
Em7/A
F♯m7/B
Emaj9
you. Ev - er, ev - er, ev - er!
you.)
Yes, I'm the one who, yes I'm the one who
(Al - ways for - ev - er love
Em7/A
F♯m7/B
Emaj9
loves you al - ways.
you.)
(Al - ways for - ev - er love
dim.
Em7/A
F♯m7/B
N.C.
Emaj9
For-ev - er, I'll love you.
you.)
freely
p

ALWAYS BE MY BABY

Words and Music by
MANUEL SEAL, JERMAINE DUPRI
and MARIAH CAREY

E
E/G♯
Amaj9
B
Cdim7
Do do do dow, do do do do do do dow.
C♯m7
E/G♯
Amaj9
F♯m7/B
Do do do dow, do do do do do do dow.
Verse:
E
B/D♯
C♯m7
G♯m
1. We were as one, babe, for a mo - ment in time.
2. I ain't gon - na cry, no, and I won't beg you to stay.
Amaj7
F♯m7
F♯m7/B
B
And it seemed ev - er - last - ing, that you would al - ways be mine.
If you're de - ter - mined to leave, boy, I will not stand in your way.

E B/D♯ C♯m7 G♯m

Now you want to be free, so I'll let you fly.
But in - ev - i - ta - bly, you'll be back a - gain.

Amaj7 F♯m7 F♯m7/B B

'Cause I know in my heart, babe, our love will nev- er die, no.
'Cause you know in your heart, babe, our love will nev- er end, no.

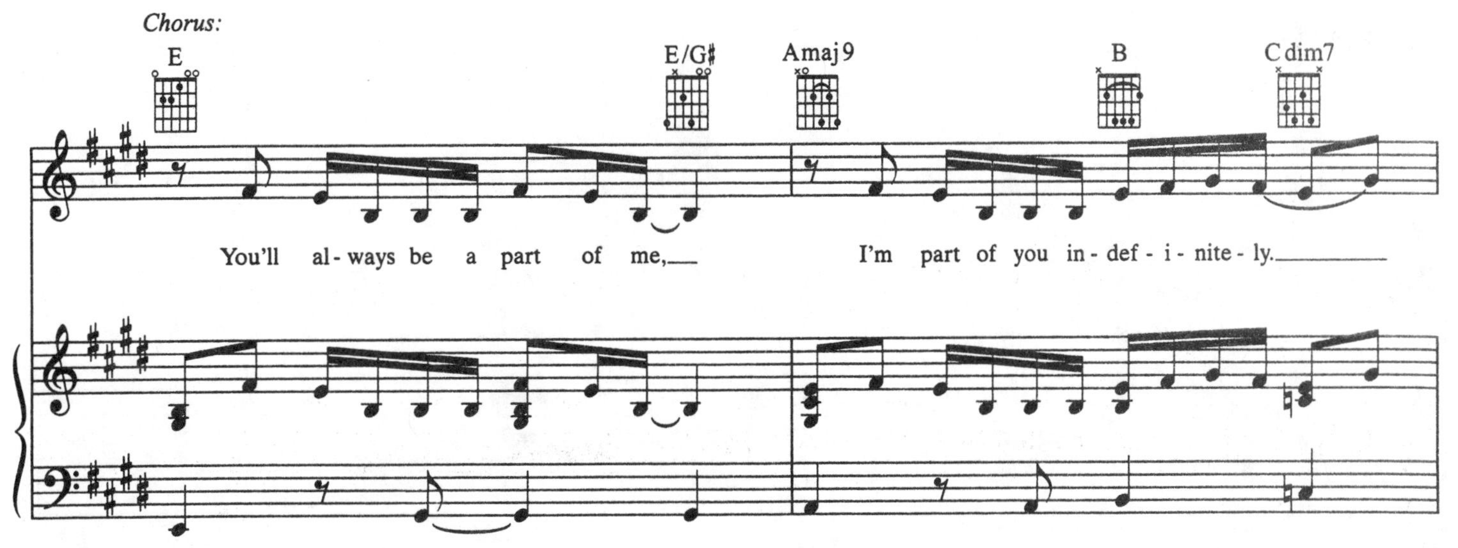
Chorus:
E E/G♯ Amaj9 B Cdim7
You'll al- ways be a part of me, I'm part of you in - def - i - nite - ly.

C♯m7
E/G♯
Amaj9
F♯m7/B
Boy, don't you know you can't es - cape me, ooh, dar - ling, 'cause you'll al - ways be my ba -
E
B
C dim7
- by. And we'll lin - ger on, time can't e - rase a feel - ing this strong.
1.
No way you're ev - er gon - na shake me, oh, dar - ling, 'cause you'll al - ways be my ba -
- by. Do do do dow, do do do do do do dow. Do do do dow,

2.
Amaj9
F♯m7/B
Amaj9
F♯m7/B
do do do do do do dow. oh, darling, 'cause you'll always be my ba-
Bridge:
C♯m7
F♯
G♯
A
G♯m
-by. I know that you'll be back, boy, when your days and your nights get a little bit
C♯m7
F♯
G♯
colder. I know that you'll be right back. Oh,
A
B
C
baby, believe me, it's only a matter of time, time.

Chorus:

F F/A B♭maj7 C D♭dim7

You'll al - ways be a part of me, I'm part of you in - def - i - nite - ly.

Dm7 F/A B♭maj7 Gm7/C

Boy, don't you know you can't es - cape me, ooh, dar - ling, 'cause you'll al - ways be my ba -

F F/A B♭maj7 C D♭dim7

- by. And we'll lin - ger on, time can't e - rase a feel - ing this strong.

Dm7 F/A B♭maj7 Gm7/C

No way you're ev - er gon - na shake me, oh, dar - ling, 'cause you'll al - ways be my ba -

F
F/A
B♭maj7
C
D♭dim7
- by. Do do do dow, do do do do do___ do dow.
Dm7
F/A
B♭maj7
Gm7/C
Do do do dow, do do do do do___ do dow.
F
F/A
B♭maj7
C
D♭dim7
Do do do dow, do do do do do___ do dow.
Dm7
F/A
B♭maj7
Gm7/C
Repeat ad lib. and fade
Do do do dow, do do do do do___ do dow.

AMAZED

Words and Music by
MARV GREEN, AIMEE MAYO
and CHRIS LINDSEY

Amazed - 4 - 1

Am7
A♭m7
F
F♭
I can hear your thoughts,
I can see your dreams.
Chorus:
D
D♭
A
A♭
I don't know how you do what you do.
I'm so in love with you.
Bm
B♭m
G
G♭
It just keeps get-ting bet - ter.
D
D♭
A
A♭
I wan - na spend the rest of my life
with you by my side
Bm
B♭m
D/A
D♭/A♭
G
G♭
for - ev - er and ev - er.

F
F♭
G
G♭
Ev - 'ry lit - tle thing that you do,
ba - by, I'm a - mazed by you.
1.
A
A♭
2.
A
A♭
C
C♭
D
D♭
A
A♭
C
C♭
G
G♭
Chorus:
Dsus
D
D♭sus
D♭
N.C.
G
G♭
A
A♭
Ev - 'ry lit - tle thing that you do,
I'm so in love with you.
Bm
B♭m
D/A
D♭/A♭
G
G♭
It just keeps get - ting bet - ter.

Verse 2:
The smell of your skin,
The taste of your kiss,
The way you whisper in the dark.
Your hair all around me,
Baby, you surround me;
You touch every place in my heart.
Oh, it feels like the first time every time.
I wanna spend the whole night in your eyes.
(To Chorus:)

ANGEL EYES

Composed by
JIM BRICKMAN

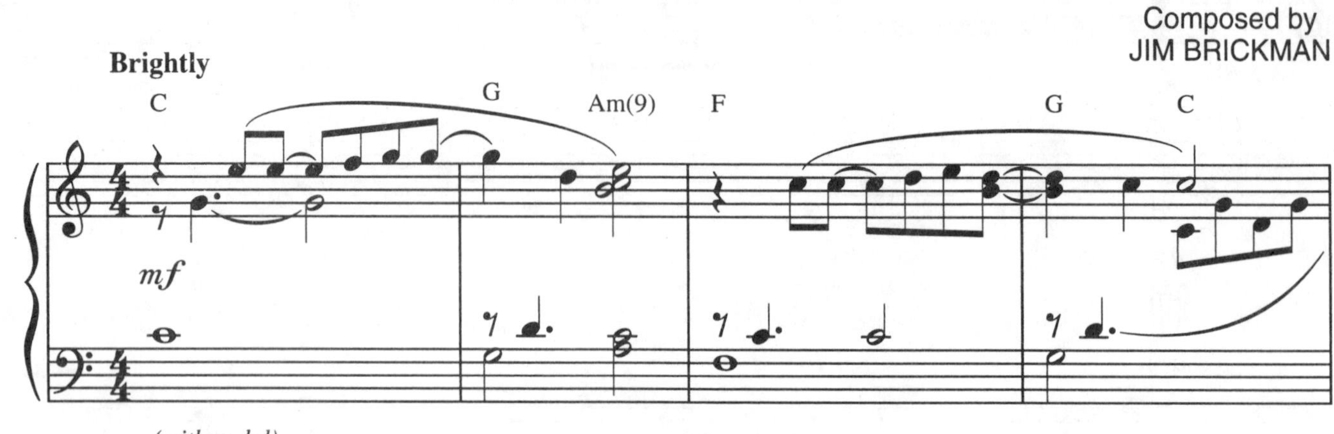

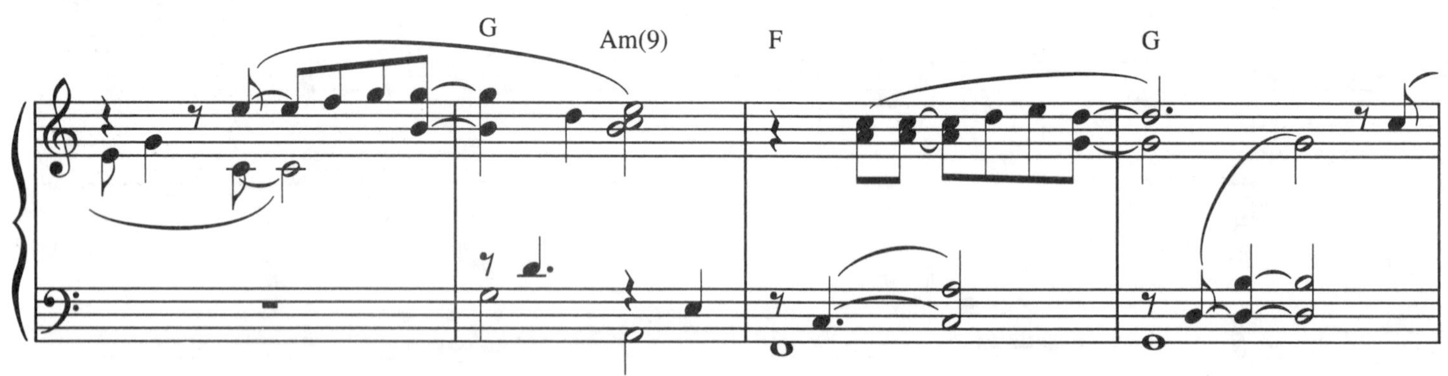

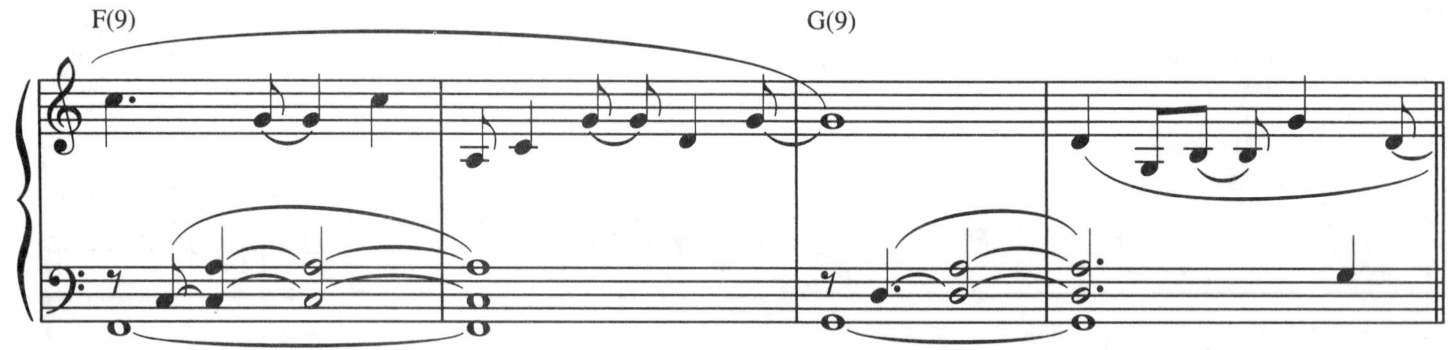

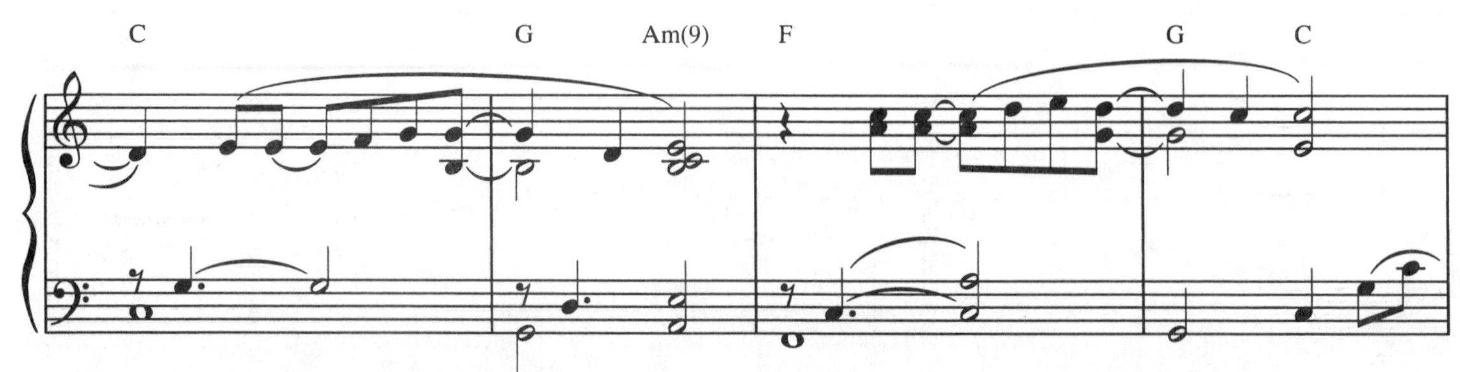

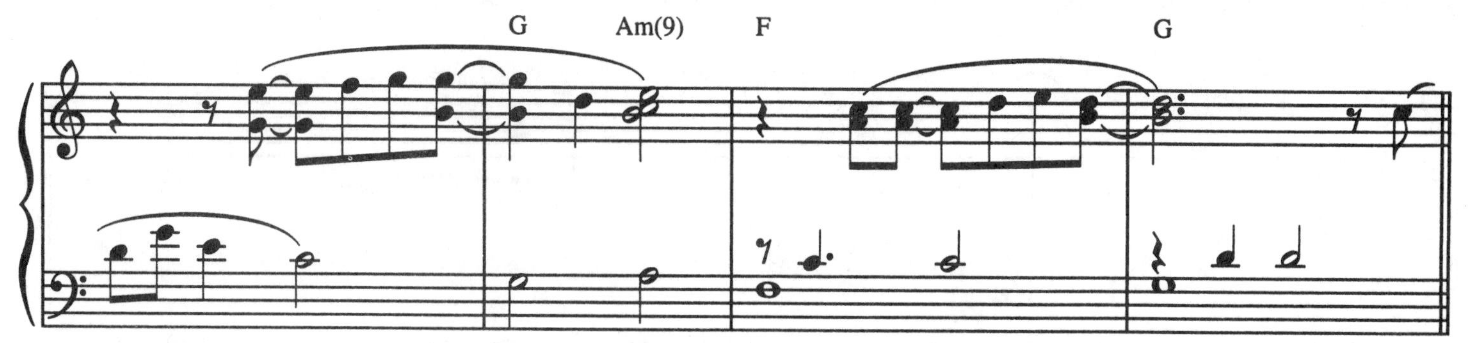
G
Am(9)
F
G

F(9)
G
Am7
F
G
C

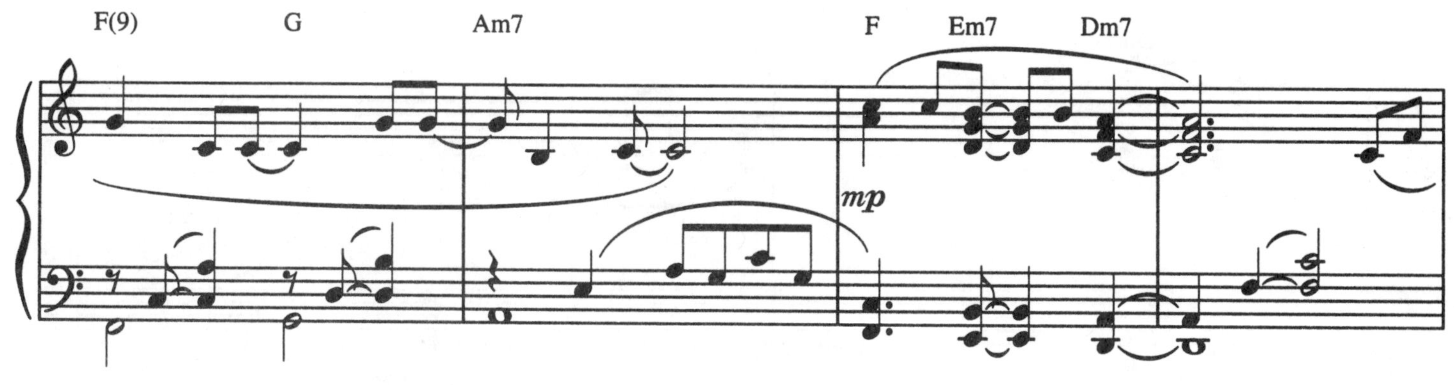
F(9)
G
Am7
F
Em7
Dm7
mp

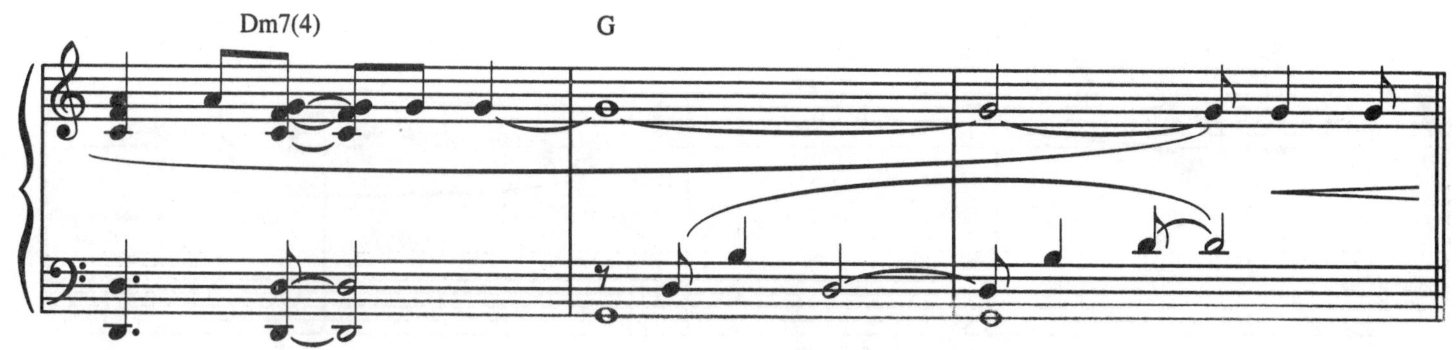
Dm7(4)
G

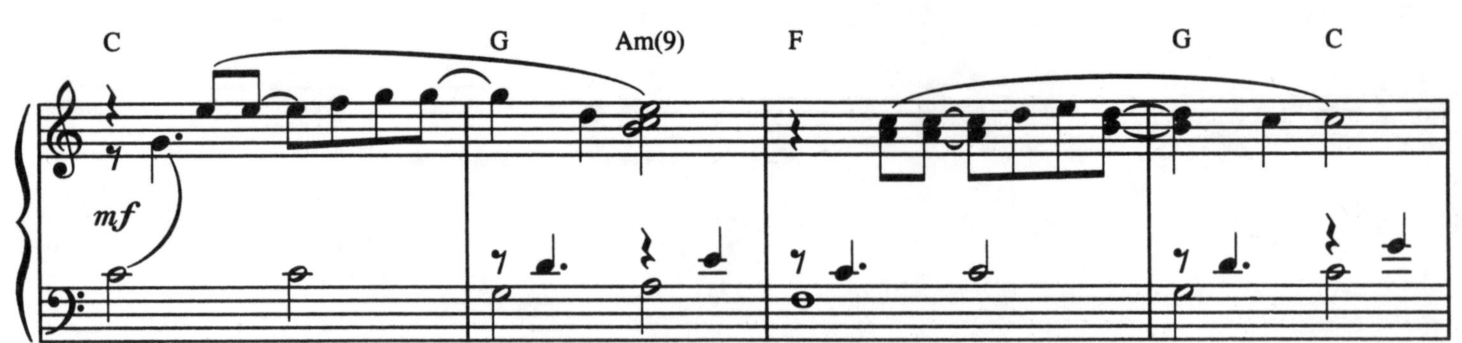
C
G
Am(9)
F
G
C
mf

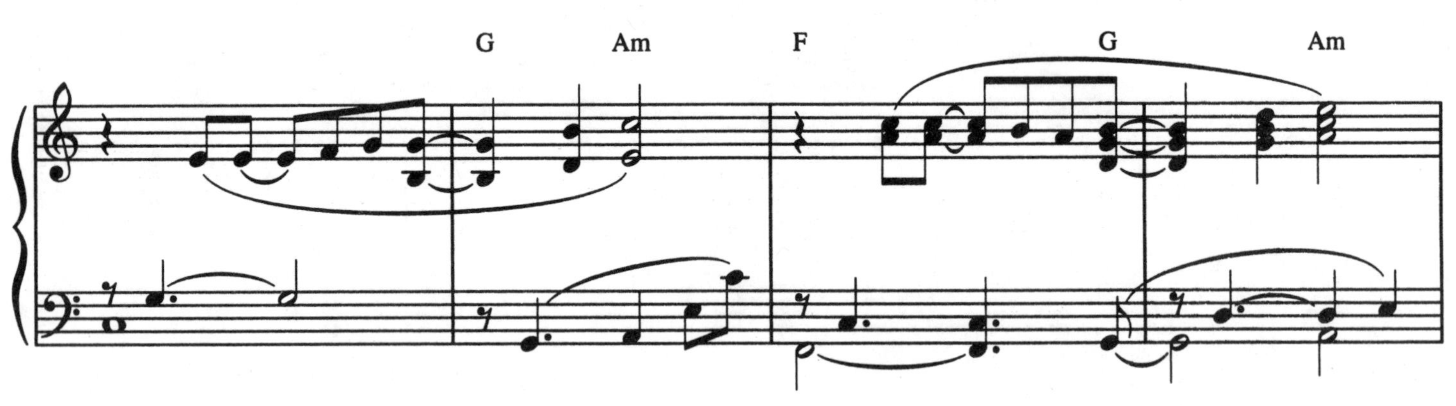
G
Am
F
G
Am

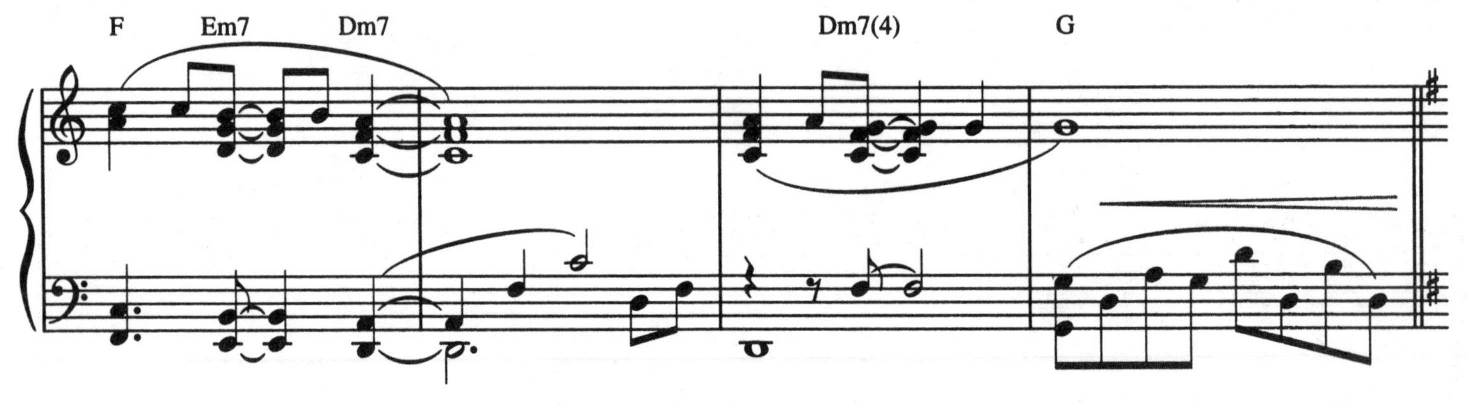
F
Em7
Dm7
Dm7(4)
G

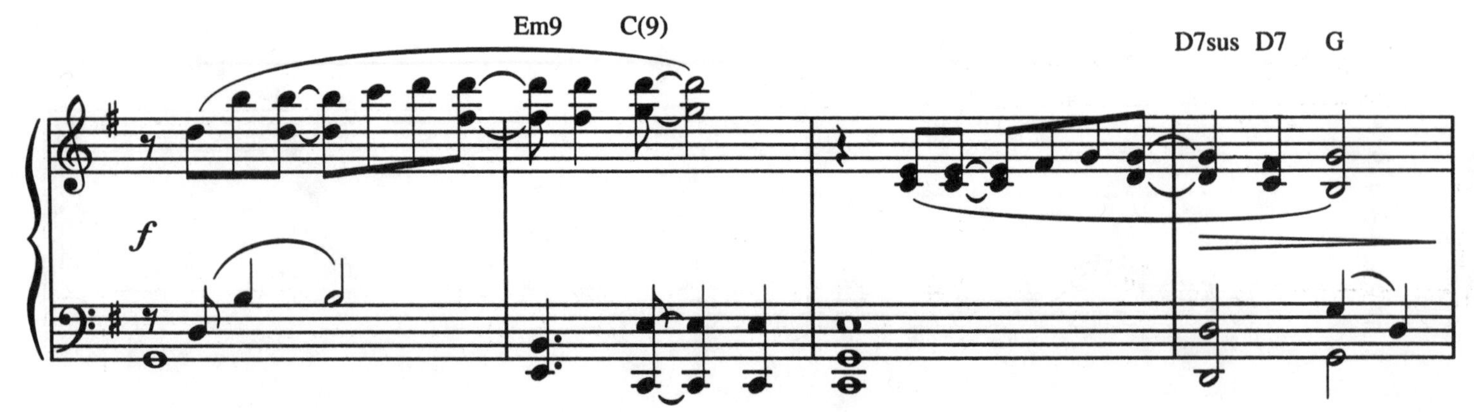
Em9
C(9)
D7sus
D7
G
f

Bm7
Cmaj9
Dsus
D
Em
mf
D
C
D/C
D
mp
G
D
Em
C
Dsus
D
G
mf
C
G
Am(9)
F
G
F(9)
G
Am7
F
G
C
mp

F(9)
G
Am7
F
Em7
Dm7
Dm7(4)
G7sus
G
C
G
Am
F
G
C
p
G
Am
F
G
mp
rit.
F(9)
Gsus
C(9)
mf
a tempo
cresc.
f

AS LONG AS YOU LOVE ME

By MAX MARTIN

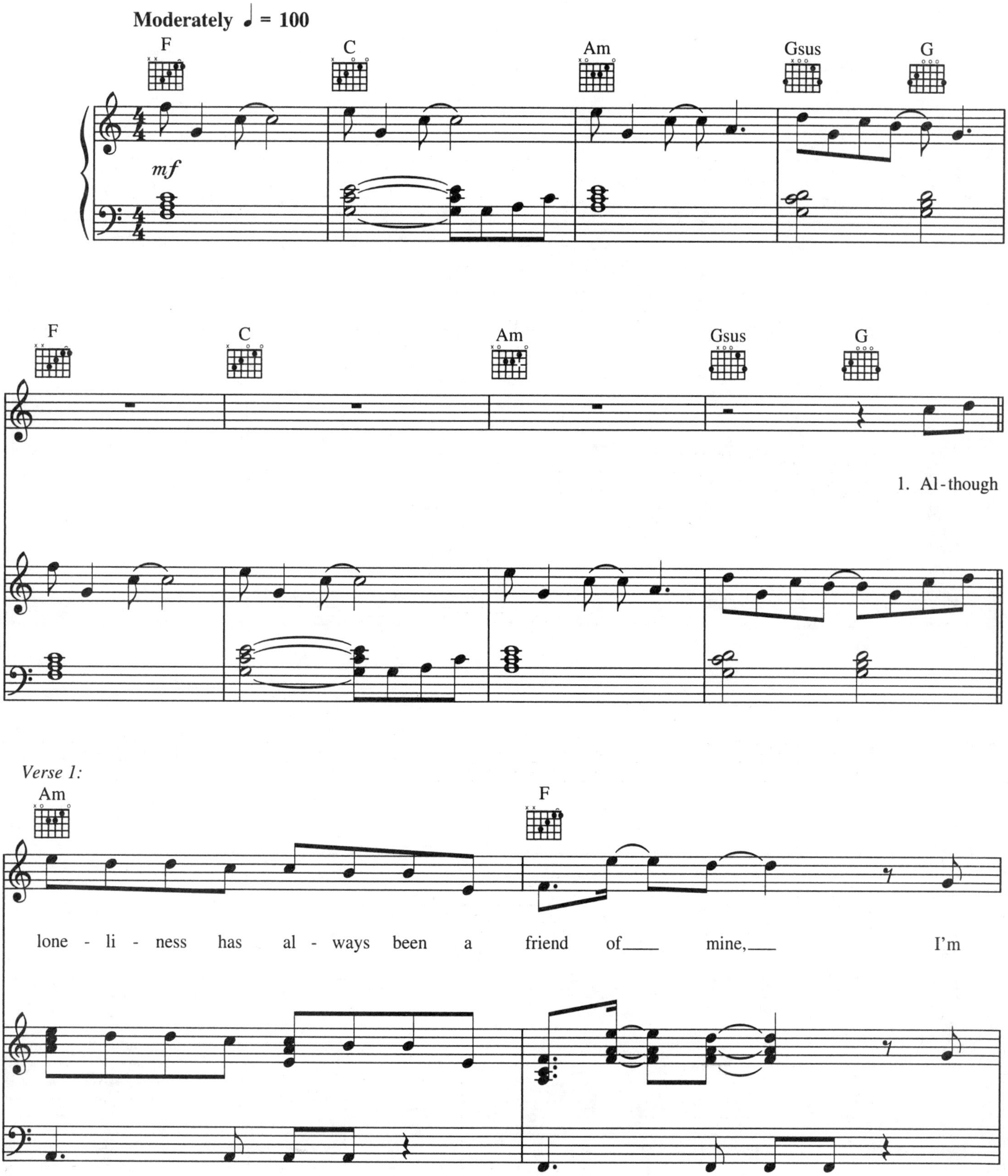

Moderately ♩ = 100

F C Am Gsus G

mf

F C Am Gsus G

1. Al-though

Verse 1:

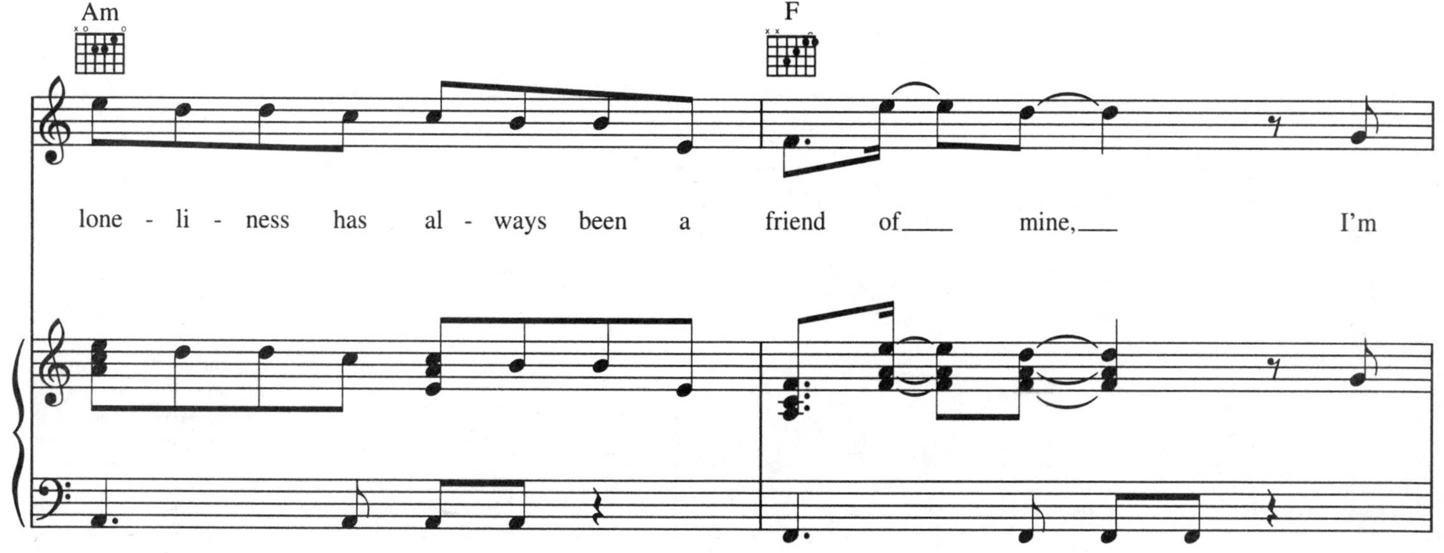
Am
F
lone - li - ness has al - ways been a friend of___ mine,___ I'm

G
C
G/B
Am
leav-ing my life in your hands.
Peo-ple say I'm cra-zy and that
F
G
C
I am blind
risk-ing it all in a glance.
Verses 2 & 3:
Am
F
2. How you got me blind is still a mys - ter - y,
I
3. Ev - 'ry lit - tle thing that you have said and done
G
C
G/B
Am
can't get you out of my head.
Don't care what is writ-ten in your
feels like it's deep with-in me.
Does-n't real-ly mat-ter if you're

F
G
C
his - to - ry
as long as you're here
with me.
on the run,
it seems like we're meant
to be.
I don't care who
Chorus:
F
C/E
Am
you are,
where you're from,
what you did,
as long
Gsus
G
F
1.
C/E
as you love me.
Who you are,
where you're from,
don't care what

2.
Am
Gsus
G
C
you did, as long as you love me.
you're from, don't care what
F
C/E
Dm
G
F
you did, as long as you love me.
C/E
Am
Gsus
G
As long as you love me.

F
C/E
Am
As long
Esus
E7
Bridge:
Am
G
as you love me.
I've tried to hide it so that no one knows, but I guess
F
G
Am
it shows when you look in - to my eyes. What you did and where you're
C/G
F♯m7(♭5)
F
G
com - ing from, I don't care, as long as you love me, ba -

F
C
Am
Gsus
G
by.
I don't care who
Chorus:
F
C/E
Am
you are, where you're from, what you did, as long
Gsus
G
F
C/E
as you love me. Who you are, where you're from, don't care what
F
C/E
Dm
G
F
you did, as long as you love me.
Who you are,

C/E
Am
Gsus
G
where_ you're from,_ what_ you did,_ as long_ as you love_
F
C/E
F
C/E
Dm
_ me. Who_ you are,_ where_ you're from,_ as long_
G
F
C/E
Dm
G
_ as you love_ me. Who_ you are,_ as long_ as you love_ me. What_
F
C/E
Dm
Gsus
G
C
_ you did,_ I don't care,_ as long_ as you love_ me._

ANGEL OF MINE

Words and Music by
RHETT LAWRENCE and TRAVON POTTS

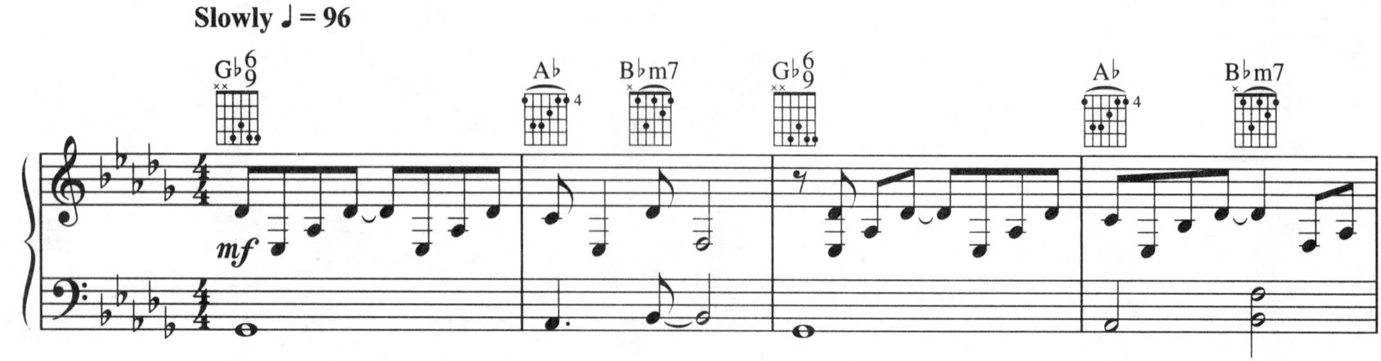

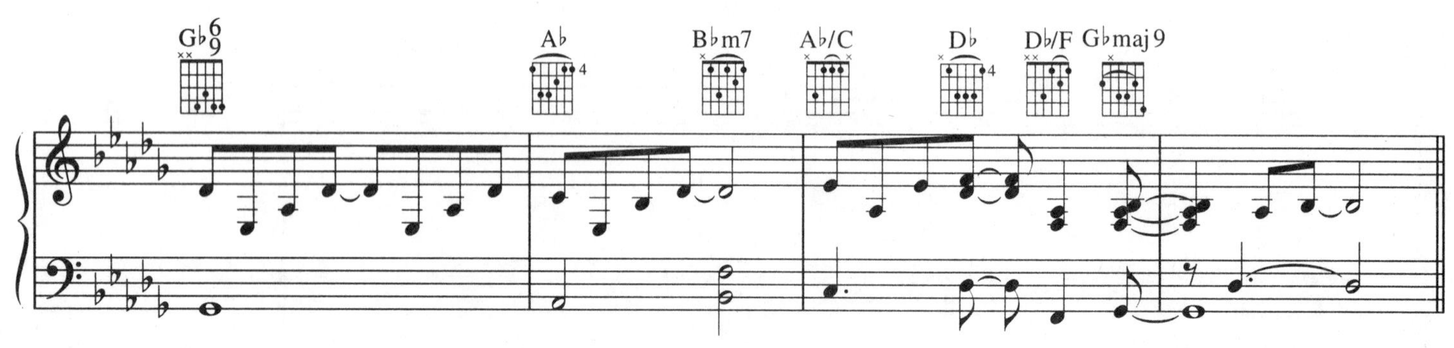

A♭ B♭m7 G♭6/9

in - side___ of you. Some - thing I thought that I would

A♭ B♭m7 A♭/C D♭ D♭/F G♭maj9

nev - er find,___ an - gel___ of mine.___

Verses 2 & 3:

G♭6/9 A♭ B♭m7

2. I look at you look - ing at me___
3. Noth - ing means more to me than what we share.___

G♭6/9 A♭ B♭m7 G♭6/9

Now I know why they say the best things_ are free.___ I'm gon - na love you, boy, you
No one in this whole world can ev - er___ com - pare.___ Last night, the way you moved is

A♭
B♭m7
A♭/C
D♭
D♭/F
G♭maj9
are so fine, an - gel of mine.
still on my mind, an - gel of mine.
Pre-chorus 1 & 2:
E♭m7
F7(♯5)
G♭(9)
1. How you changed my world, you'll nev - er know. I'm dif-f'rent now, you
2. What you mean to me, you'll nev - er know. Deep in - side I
C♭
Chorus:
G♭6/9
A♭
B♭m7
helped me grow.
need to show.
You came in - to my life straight from a - bove.
G♭6/9
A♭
B♭m7
G♭6/9
When I lost all hope, you showed me love. I'm check-ing for you, boy, you're

To Coda
Ab
Bbm7
Ab/C
Db
Db/F
Gbmaj9
1.
right on time,
an - gel of mine.
2.
Bridge:
Ab7sus
Ab
I nev - er knew I could feel each mo - ment
F7/A
F7(b9)
Bbm7
Gb9
as if it were new.
Ev - 'ry breath that I take, the love
Ab/C
F7
Bbm7
Ab/C
Db
Bb7
Ab7/C
Bb7/D
that we make,
I on - ly share it with you,
you, you, you.

Verse 4:
G♭6/9
A♭
B♭m7
G♭6/9
4. When I first saw you, I al - read - y knew there was some-thing
A♭
B♭m7
G♭6/9
A♭
B♭m7
in - side of you. Some-thing I thought that I would nev - er find,
A♭/C
D♭
D♭/F
G♭maj 9
D.S.% al Coda
an - gel of mine. You
Coda
Pre-chorus 3:
E♭m7
F 7(♯5)
3. How you changed my world, you'll nev - er know.

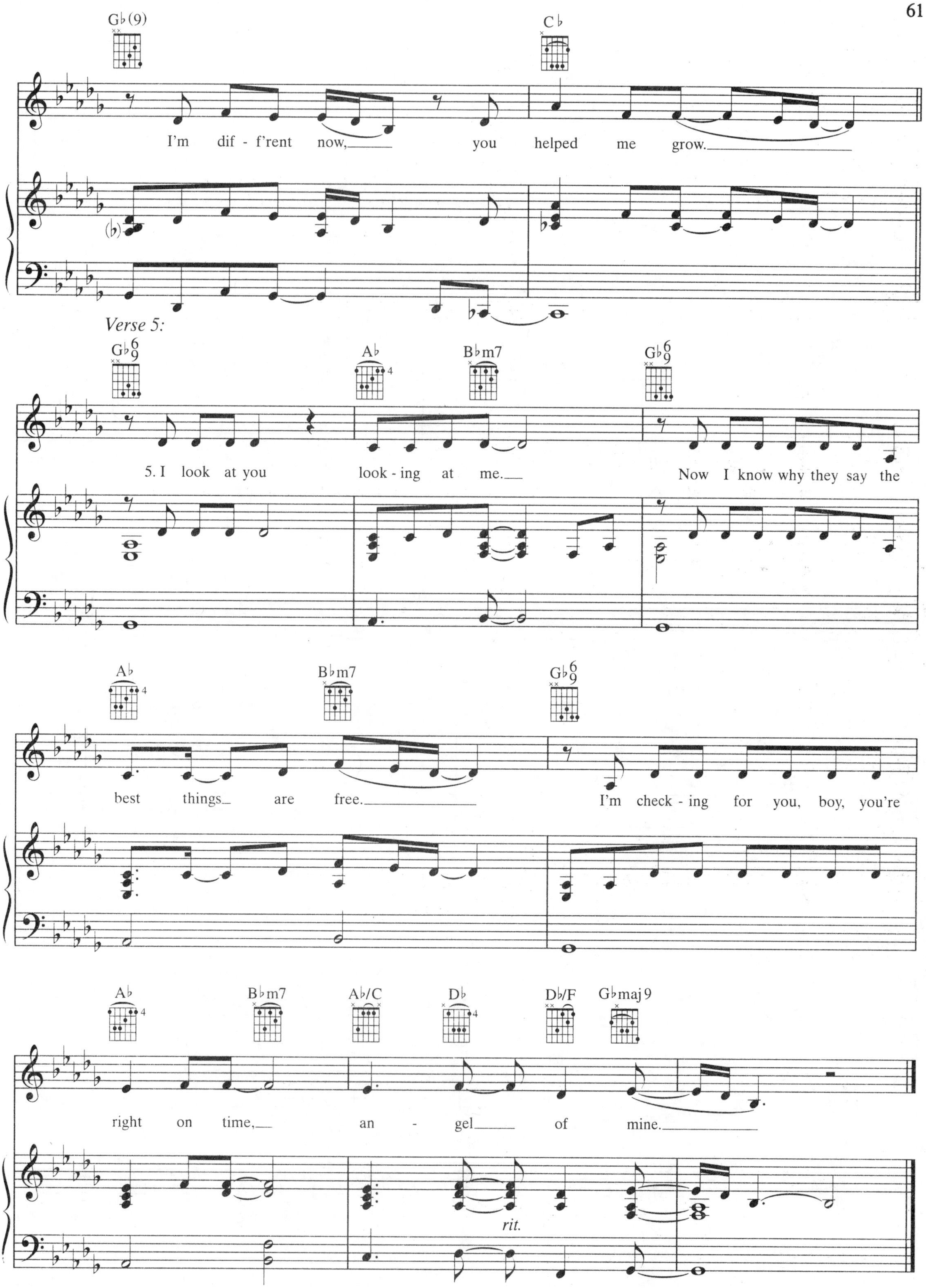

G♭(9) C♭

I'm dif - f'rent now, you helped me grow.

Verse 5:

G♭6/9 A♭ B♭m7 G♭6/9

5. I look at you look - ing at me. Now I know why they say the

A♭ B♭m7 G♭6/9

best things are free. I'm check - ing for you, boy, you're

A♭ B♭m7 A♭/C D♭ D♭/F G♭maj9

right on time, an - gel of mine.

rit.

BACK AT ONE

Words and Music by
BRIAN McKNIGHT
Slowly ♩ = 72
Verse:
B(9)
G♯m7
1. It's un - de - ni - a - ble that we should be to - geth - er.
2. It's so in - cred - i - ble, the way things work them - selves out.
E(9)
C♯m7
D♯m7
E
F♯
It's un - be - liev - a - ble how I used to say that I'd fall nev - er.
And all e - mo - tion - al, once you know what it's all a - bout, hey.
B(9)
G♯m7
The ba - sis is need to know. If you don't know just how I feel, then
And un - de - sir - a - ble, for us to be a - part. I

Amaj7
E(9)/G♯
C♯/E♯
let me show you now that I'm for real. If
nev - er would have made it ver - y far, 'cause you
Amaj7
E(9)/G♯
C♯m7/F♯
all things in time, time will re - veal. Yeah.
know you've got the keys to my heart. 'Cause
Chorus:
B
G♯m7
F♯sus
One, one, you're like a dream come true. Two, just wan - na be with you.
E(9)
C♯m7
D♯m7
E
F♯
Three, girl, it's plain to see that you're the on - ly one for me. And

B
G♯m7
F♯sus
four, re - peat steps one through three. Five, make you fall in love with me. If
E(9)
C♯m7
C♯m7/F♯
ev - er I be - lieve my work is done, then I'll start back at one.
B
C♯m7
C♯m7/F♯
E
Yeah.
Say
then I'll start back at one.
Bridge:
B/D♯
E(9)
fare - well to the dark of night; I see the com - ing of the sun. I

B/D♯
G♯sus
G♯7(♯5)
feel like a lit - tle child whose life has just be - gun. You
C♯m7
D♯m7
G♯m7
came and breathed new life in - to this lone - ly heart of mine. You
C♯m7
C♯m7/F♯
Dm7/G G/B
N.C.
threw out the life - line, just in the nick of time.
Chorus:
C
Am7
Gsus
One, you're like a dream come true. Two, just wan - na be with you.

F(9)
C/E
Dm7
Em7
F
G
Three, girl, it's plain to see that you're the on - ly one___ for me.___ And
C
Am7
Gsus
four, re - peat steps one through three. Five, make you fall in love with me. If
F(9)
Dm7
Dm7/G
ev - er I___ be - lieve___ my work___ is done,___ then I'll start___ back___ at one.___
C
F
Am11
Dm11
Dm7/G
Amaj9
rit.

BECAUSE YOU LOVE ME

Because You Love Me - 3 - 1

Verses 2, 3, & 5:
A
F♯m
E
C♯7/E♯
call what I've been through, there's some
3.5. See additional lyrics
F♯m
C♯m
D
things that I wish I didn't do. And now I do the things I
To Coda
A/E
E
Bm/A
A
D/A
A
do because you love me. And now that
cresc.
Bridge:
D
C♯m
you're in my life, I'm so glad I'm a - live;
mf
C♯7/E♯
F♯m
C♯
'cause you showed me the way. And I know now how good it can

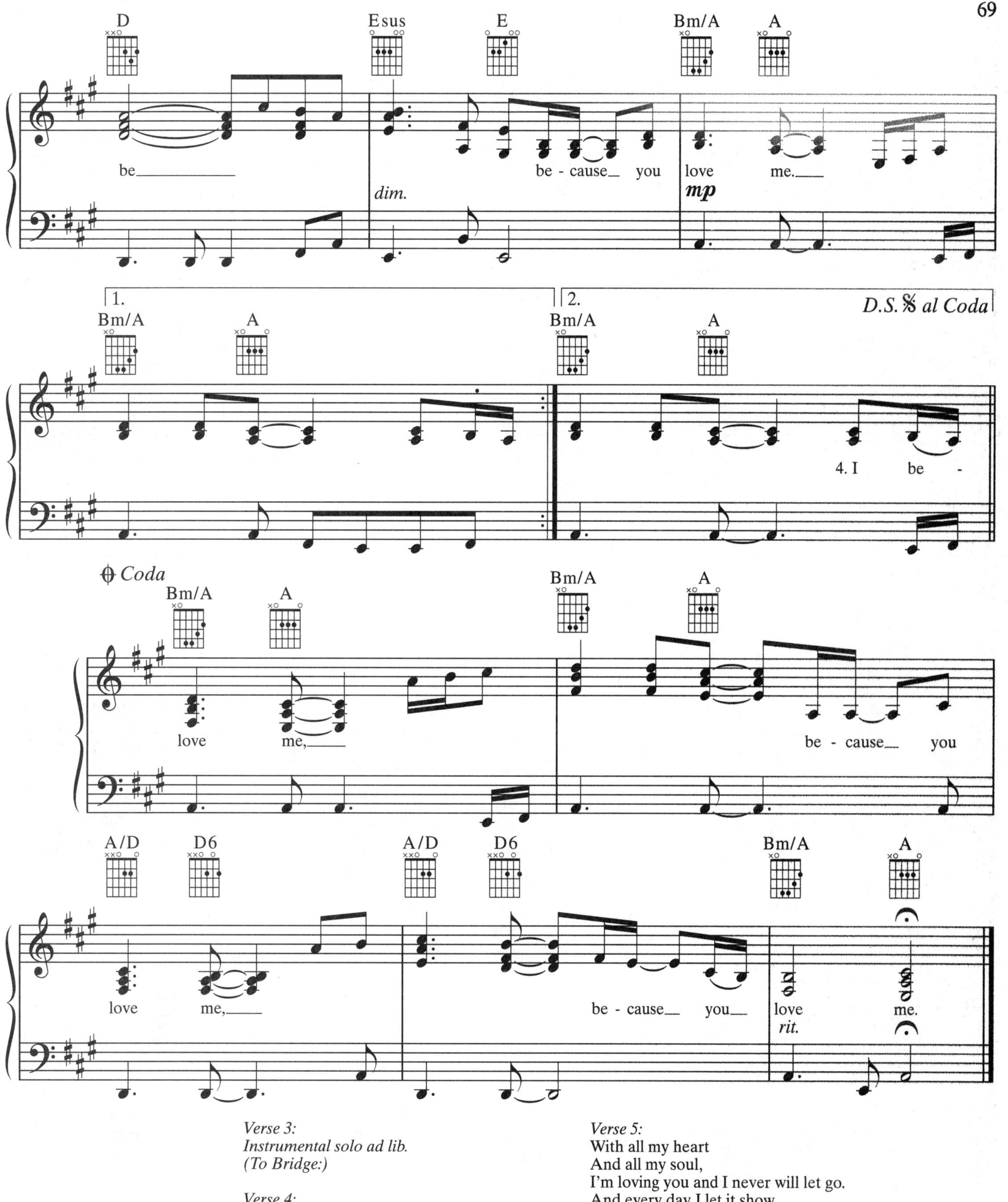

Verse 3:
Instrumental solo ad lib.
(To Bridge:)

Verse 4:
I believe in things unseen;
I believe in the message of a dream.
And I believe in what you are
Because you love me.

Verse 5:
With all my heart
And all my soul,
I'm loving you and I never will let go.
And every day I let it show
Because you love me.
(To Coda)

BECAUSE YOU LOVED ME
(Theme from "Up Close & Personal")

Words and Music by
DIANE WARREN

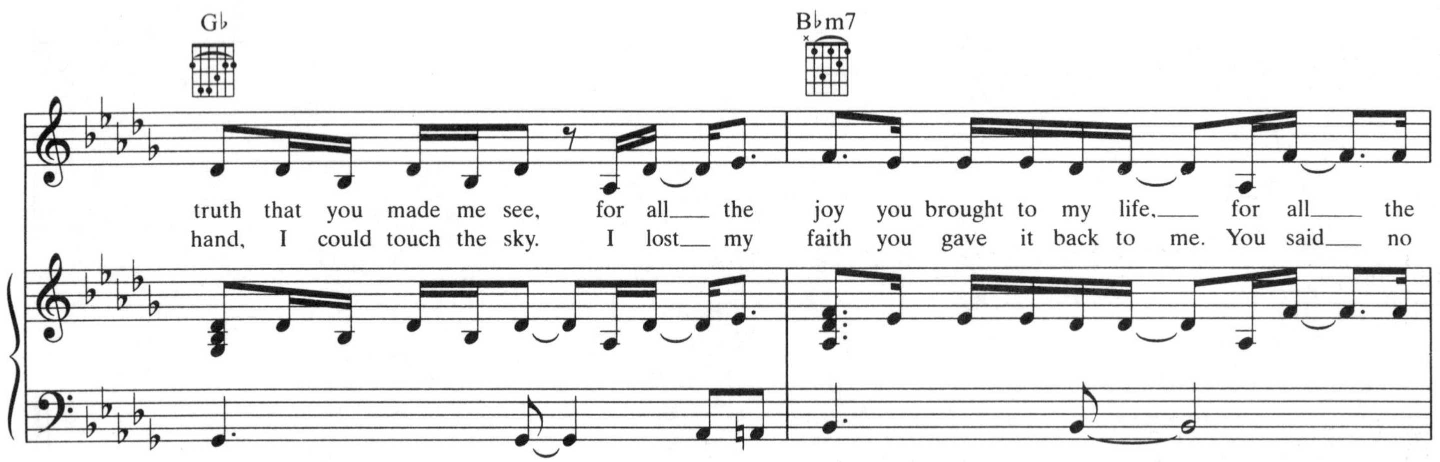

G♭maj7
E♭m7/A♭
love I found in you, I'll be for-ev-er thank-ful, ba-by.
love, I had it all. I'm grate-ful for each day you gave me.
C♭6
B♭m7
E♭m7
You're the one who held me up, never let me fall.
May-be I don't know that much, but I know this much is true.
G♭m7
E♭m7/A♭
You're the one who saw me through, through it all.
I was blessed be-cause I was loved by you.
You were my
Chorus:
D♭
G♭
strength when I was weak, you were my voice when I could-n't speak. You were my

B♭m7
A♭sus
A♭
eyes when I could-n't see, you saw_ the best there was_ in me, lift-ed_ me_
Fm7
G♭maj9
C♭maj7
up when I could-n't reach. You gave_me faith 'coz you_ be-lieved._ I'm
E♭m7/A♭
To Coda
1.
D♭
E♭m7/A♭
ev-ery-thing_ I am be-cause_ you loved_ me. 2. You gave_ me
2.
D♭
Bridge:
F7/A
B♭m7
loved_ me. You were al-ways there_for me, the ten-der wind_ that car-ried_ me. A

F 7/A
B♭m7
light in the dark, shin - ing your love in - to my life. You've
E♭m7
D♭/F
been my in - spi - ra - tion, through the lies, you were the truth. My
E♭m7/A♭
D.S. 𝄋 al Coda
world is a bet - ter place be - cause of you. You were my
Coda
D♭
Fm7/B♭
E♭
loved me. You were my strength when I was weak, you were my

A♭
Cm7
voice when I could-n't speak. You were my eyes when I could-n't see, you saw the
B♭sus
Gm7
best there was in me, lift-ed me up when I could-n't reach. You gave me
A♭maj9
D♭maj7
Fm7/B♭
faith 'coz you be-lieved. I'm ev-ery-thing I am be-cause you
E♭
Fm7/B♭
E♭
loved me. I'm ev-ery-thing I am be-cause you loved me.

BREATHE

Words and Music by
HOLLY LAMAR and STEPHANIE BENTLEY

Am7 G/B C(9) G/B
I watch the sun - light dance a - cross your face and I've
Am7 Dsus
nev - er been this swept a - way.
Verses 2 & 3:
Am7 G/B C(9) G/B
2. All my thoughts just seem to set - tle on the breeze
3. In a way, I know my heart is wak - ing up
Am7 G/B C(9)
when I'm ly - in' wrapped up in your arms.
as all the walls come tum - blin' down.
Am7 G/B C(9) G/B
The whole world just fades a - way, the on - ly thing I
Clos-er than I've ev - er felt be - fore and I know and you know

Am7
D
D7
hear is the beat - ing of your heart.
there's no need for words right now.
cresc.
'Cause I can feel you
mf
Chorus:
G
Am7
C (9)
D7sus
D7
breathe, it's wash-ing o - ver me and sud-den - ly I'm melt - in' in - to you. There's noth-in' left to
G
Am7
C (9)
D7sus
D7
prove, ba - by, all we need is just to be caught up in the
G
Am7
C (9)
G/B
touch, the slow and stead-y rush. And ba - by, is - n't that the way that love's sup - posed
Am7
D7sus
D7
to be?
I can feel you
dim.
mp

1.
C (9)
G/B
Am7
D7sus
G
Am7
breathe.
cresc.
mf
Just
breathe.
C (9)
Dsus
D
G
Am7
C (9)
Dsus
2.
C (9)
G/B
Am7
D7sus
breathe.
cresc.
mf
Just
G
Am7
C (9)
Dsus
D
G
Am7
breathe.
C (9)
D7sus
G
Am7
Caught up in the touch, the slow and stead-y rush. And ba-by, is-n't

C(9)
G/B
Am7
D7sus
D7
that the way that love's sup - posed to be?
dim.
mp
I can feel you
G
breathe.
Just breathe.
I can feel the mag - ic float - ing in
the air;
be - ing with you gets me that way.
rit.

BUTTERFLY KISSES

Words and Music by
BOB CARLISLE and RANDY THOMAS

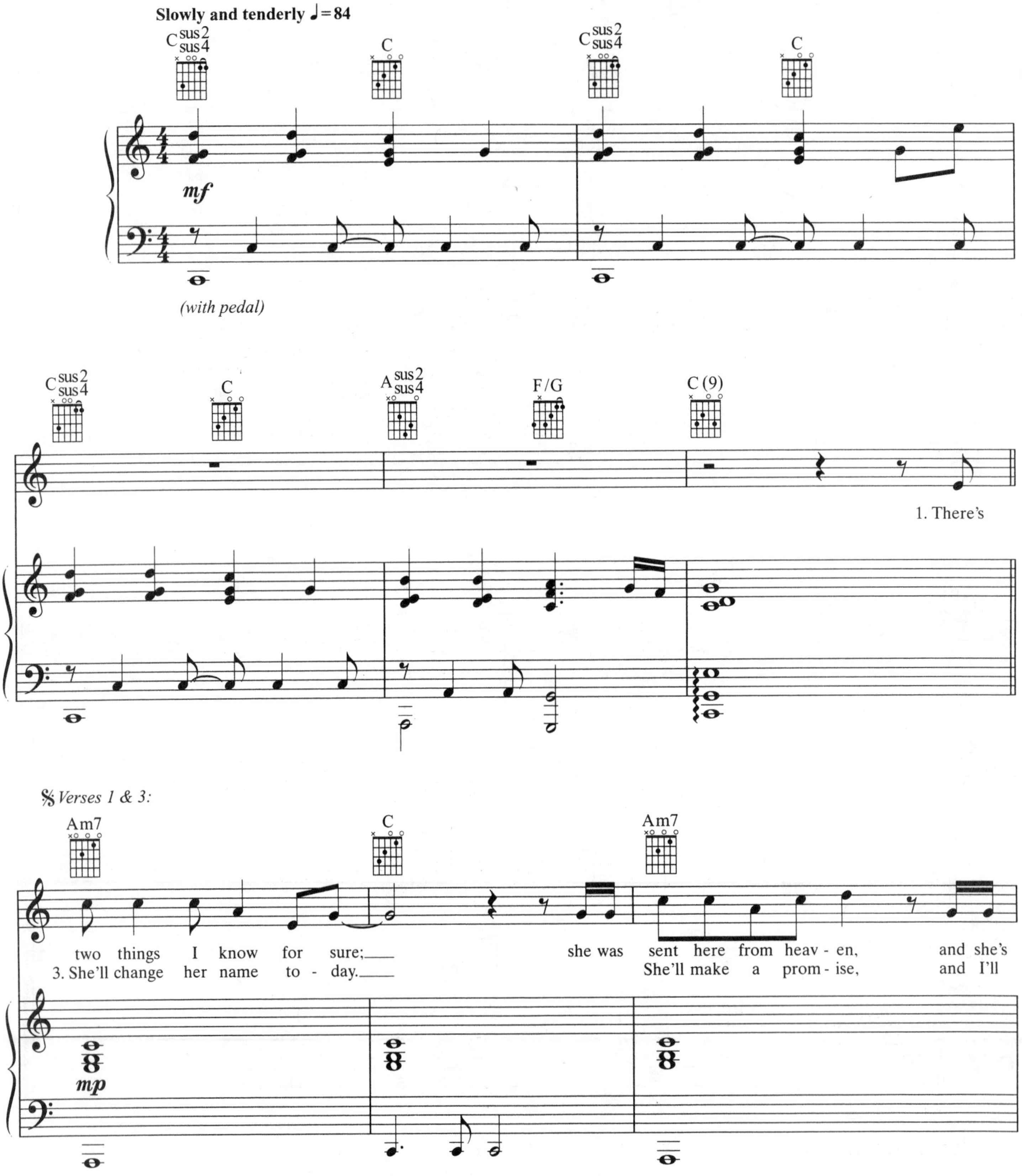

Slowly and tenderly ♩= 84
Csus2 sus4
C
Csus2 sus4
C
mf
(with pedal)
Csus2 sus4
C
Asus2 sus4
F/G
C(9)
1. There's
Verses 1 & 3:
Am7
C
Am7
two things I know for sure; she was sent here from heav - en, and she's
3. She'll change her name to - day. She'll make a prom - ise, and I'll
mp

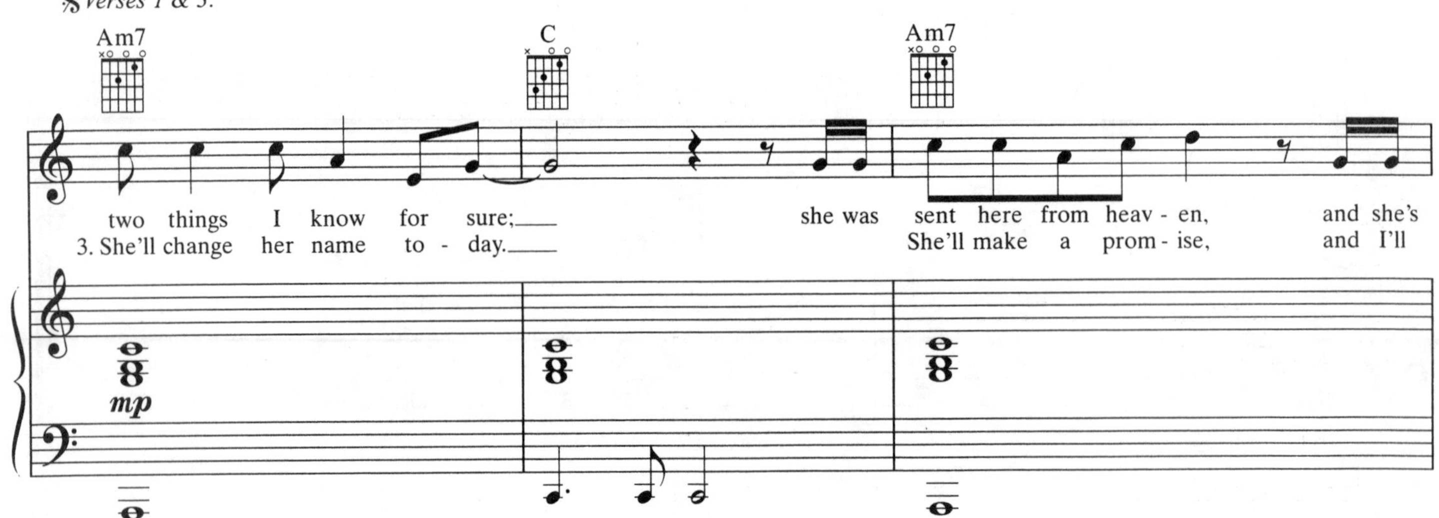

C
Dm7
C/E
F sus 2 sus 4
Gsus
G
dad - dy's lit - tle girl. As I drop to my knees by her bed at night,
give her a - way. Stand - ing in the bride room just star - ing at her, she
Dm7
C/E
F sus 2 sus 4
Gsus
G
F(9)/A
G/B
3
3
she talks to Je - sus, and I close my eyes. And I thank God for all of the
asks me what I'm think - ing, and I say, "I'm not sure. I just feel like I'm los - ing my
C
F(9)/A
F/G
joy in my life, oh, but most of all, for
ba - by girl." Then she leaned o - ver and gave me
Chorus 1 & 3:
C sus 2 sus 4
C
C sus 2 sus 4
C
but - ter - fly kiss - es af - ter bed - time prayer, stick - in'
but - ter - fly kiss - es with her ma - ma there, stick - in'
mf

Csus2 sus4
C
G/C
Asus2 sus4
Am
G
lit - tle white flow - ers all up in her hair.
lit - tle white flow - ers all up in her hair.
F(9)
C/E
"Walk be - side the po - ny, dad - dy, it's my first ride." "I
"Walk me down the aisle, dad - dy, it's just a - bout time." "Does my
F(9)
C/E
know the cake looks fun - ny, dad - dy, but I sure tried." Oh, with
wed - ding gown look pret - ty, dad - dy?" "Dad - dy, don't cry." Oh, with
F/A
G/B
C
Dsus
D
To Coda
all that I've done wrong, I must have done some - thing right to de - serve a
all that I've done wrong, I must have done some - thing right to de - serve her

F(9)
G7sus
Csus2 sus4
C
C(9)
hug ev-'ry morn - ing and but-ter-fly kiss-es at night.
mp
p
Verse 2:
Am7
C
Am7
2. Sweet six - teen to - day; she's look-ing like her ma - ma a lit-tle
3
mp
C
Dm7
C/E
F6 9
Gsus
G
more ev - 'ry day. One part wom - an, the oth-er part girl; to
Dm7
C/E
F(9)
G7sus
G
F(9)/A
G/B
per-fume and make - up from rib-bons and curls; try-ing her wings out in a

C(9)
F(9)/A
Gsus
great big world. But I re - mem - ber
Chorus 2:
Csus2 sus4
C
but-ter-fly kiss-es af-ter bed-time prayer, stick-in' lit-tle white flow - ers all
mf
G/C
Asus2 sus4
Am
G
F(9)
up in her hair. "You know how much I love you, dad - dy, but if
C/E
you don't mind, I'm on-ly gon - na kiss you on the cheek this time." Oh, with

F/A
G/B
C
Dsus
D
all that I've done wrong, I must have done some-thing right to de-serve her
F(9)
G7sus
Csus2 sus4
C
Csus2 sus4
C
love ev-'ry morn-ing and but-ter-fly kiss-es at night.
(All the pre-cious
cresc.
Bridge:
E♭
Dm
Csus2 sus4
C
Csus2 sus4
C
time.)
Oh, like the wind, the years go by.
(Pre-cious but-ter-
f
E♭
Dm7
F/A
G
D.S. 𝄋 al Coda
fly, spread your wings and fly.)
dim.

Coda
F(9)
G7sus
F(9)/A
love ev-'ry morn - ing and but-ter-fly kiss-es. I could-n't ask God for more, man,
G/B
A♭maj 9
C/G
poco rit.
this is what love is. I know I've got to let her go, but I'll al - ways re-mem-ber
poco rit.
freely
F(9)
G7sus
ev-'ry hug in the morn - ing and but-ter-fly kiss - es.
freely
a tempo
Csus2 sus4
C
G/A
G7sus
C(9)
a tempo
rit. e dim.
mp

YOU WERE MEANT FOR ME

G/B
C
D
pan-cakes, too,
I've got ma-ple syr-up,
ev-'ry - thing but
you.
C(9)
G/B
C
I break the yolks and make a
smil-y
face,
I kind of like it in my
Em
C(9)
G/B
brand new
place.
I wipe the
spots a - bove the mirror, don't leave the
keys in the
door.
I
C
D
Chorus:
C
nev-er put wet
towels
on the
floor an - y - more, 'cause...
Dreams last
for

D
G
D/F♯
Em7
G/D
so long,
e - ven af - ter you're gone.
C
D
G
D/F♯
I know
you love me and
soon you will see
Em7
G/D
C
To Coda
1.
D
you were meant for me
and I was meant for you.
Em
2.
D
I was meant for

Em
Bridge:
Am7
you.
I go a-bout my bus-'ness, I'm
D
Bm
D
Em7
do-in' fine. Be-sides, what would I say if I had you on the line?
Am7
D
Bm7
Em
Same old sto-ry, not much to say. Hearts are bro-ken ev-'ry day.
C (9)
G/B
C
Em
D.S. al Coda

Verse 2:
I called my mama, she was out for a walk.
Consoled a cup of coffee, but it didn't wanna talk.
So I picked up a paper, it was more bad news,
More hearts being broken or people being used.
Put on my coat in the pouring rain.
I saw a movie, it just wasn't the same,
'Cause it was happy and I was sad,
And it made me miss you, oh, so bad.
(To Chorus:)

Verse 3:
I brush my teeth and put the cap back on,
I know you hate it when I leave the light on.
I pick a book up and then I turn the sheets down,
And then I take a breath and a good look around.
Put on my pj's and hop into bed.
I'm half alive but I feel mostly dead.
I try and tell myself it'll be all right,
I just shouldn't think anymore tonight.
(To Chorus:)

BY HEART

Composed by
JIM BRICKMAN and
HOLLYE LEVEN

Slowly ♩ = 63

Verse:

F(9) F B♭ Dm(9)

1. Hold me close, ba - by, please.
2. When you go, I'll stop the clock.

mp

(with pedal)

E♭(9) F(9) F B♭ Dm(9)

Tell me an-y-thing but that you're gon - na leave.
I won't ev - er let this mo - ment stop.

E♭(9) F B♭ Dm(9) B♭(9)

As I kiss this fall - en tear, I
Time is steal - in' you from me, but it can

Gm7(4)
C7sus
C
prom - ise you I will be here.
nev - er take this mem - o - ry.
Un - til the stars
Chorus:
B♭
C
F
B♭
C
F
3
fall from the sky, un - til I find a rea - son why, and, dar-ling,
3
E♭
C
as the years go by, un - til there's no

B♭
C
F
B♭
C
Dm
tears left to cry, until the an - gels close my eyes
mf
Gm7
F/A
Am7/D
D
and e - ven if we're worlds a - part, I'll
Gm7
C7sus
C
To Coda
find my way back to you by heart.
mp
1.
F
Dm
Gm7
C7sus
C

2.
F
Dm
Gm7
C
D.S. 𝄋 al Coda
F
Dm
Gm7
C7sus
C
Un-til the stars
Coda
F
Dm
Gm7
C
F
Dm
Gm7
C7sus
C7
F
rit. e dim.
p

CAN'T NOBODY LOVE YOU (LIKE I DO)

Words and Music by
DANNY ORTON and CATHY MAJESKI

Gm7
Eb(9)
Gm7
Oth - ers may prom - ise the stars in the sky, but soon - er or lat -
Eb(9)
Fsus
F
Abmaj7
Eb
er you'll find, can't no - bod - y love you like I
1.
Bb(9)
Bb(9)/D
Eb
Gm7
do.
Bb(9)/D
Eb(9)
2.
Bb
Abmaj7
Eb
do. Can't no - bod - y love you like I
Bb
Bb(9)/D
Eb(9)
do.
Well,

Bridge:
A♭
E♭
Cm7
B♭
A♭
Cm7
who knows when it's meant to be.
Love knows, and it
E♭
Fsus
F
Verse 3:
D♭
sent you to me.
(Instrumental)
G♭
A♭sus
A♭
D♭
B♭m
G♭(9)
You don't know how I live for the day
B♭m
G♭(9)
A♭sus
A♭
C♭maj7
G♭
you look at me and you say: "Can't no-bod-y love you like I

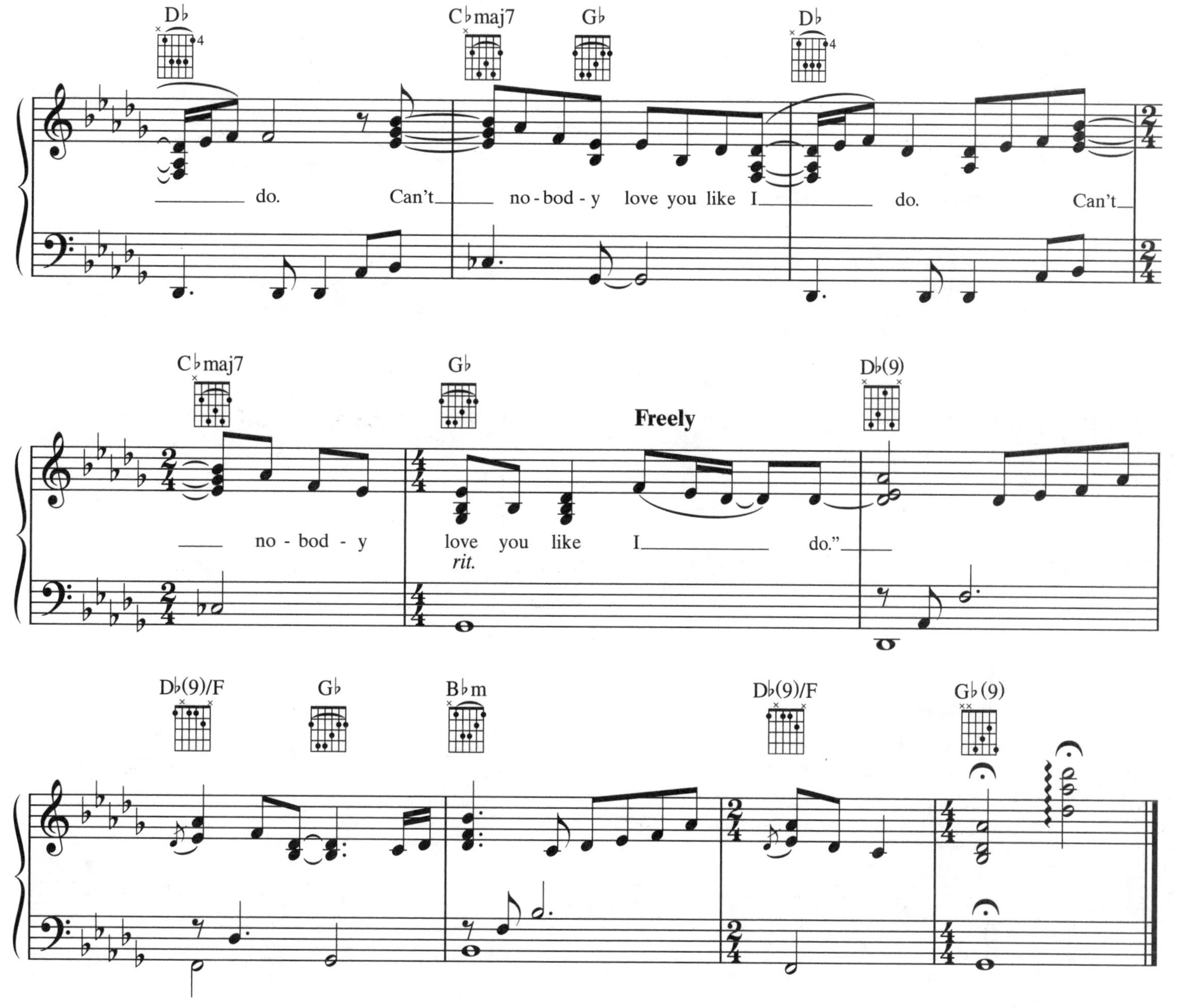

Verse 2:
Can't nobody hold you quite this close
All night like I want to.
Baby, put your sweet lips here on mine.
You'll see, 'cause I'm gonna show you
Just how an angel like you should be loved.
Man, I can't feel you enough.
Can't nobody love you like I do.
Can't nobody love you like I do.

DREAMING OF YOU

Words and Music by
TOM SNOW and
FRANNE GOLDE

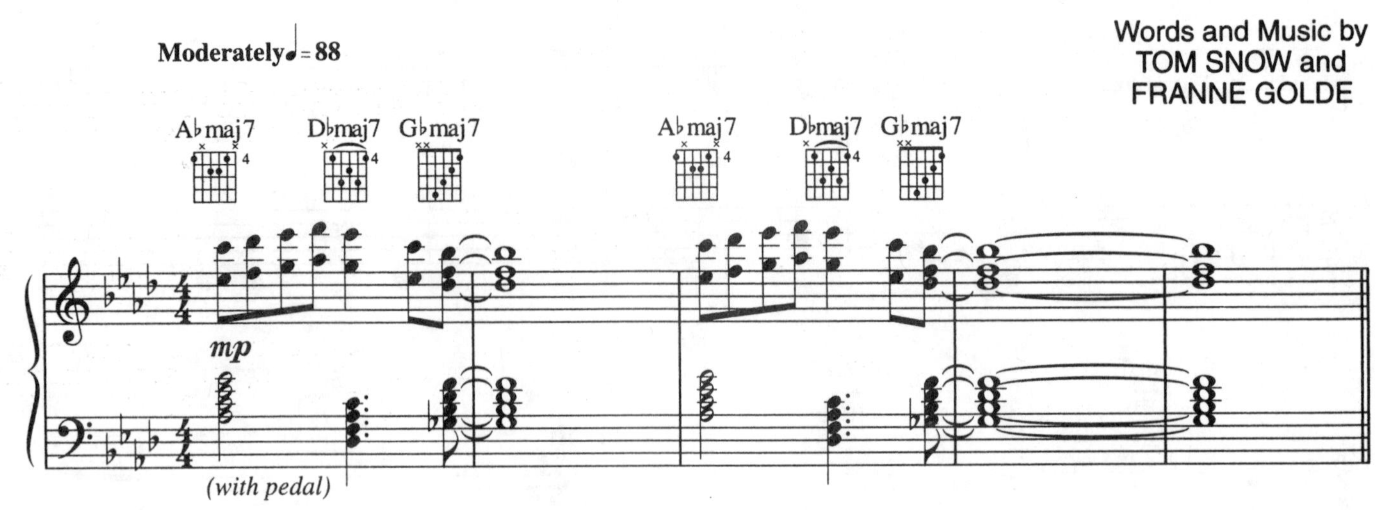

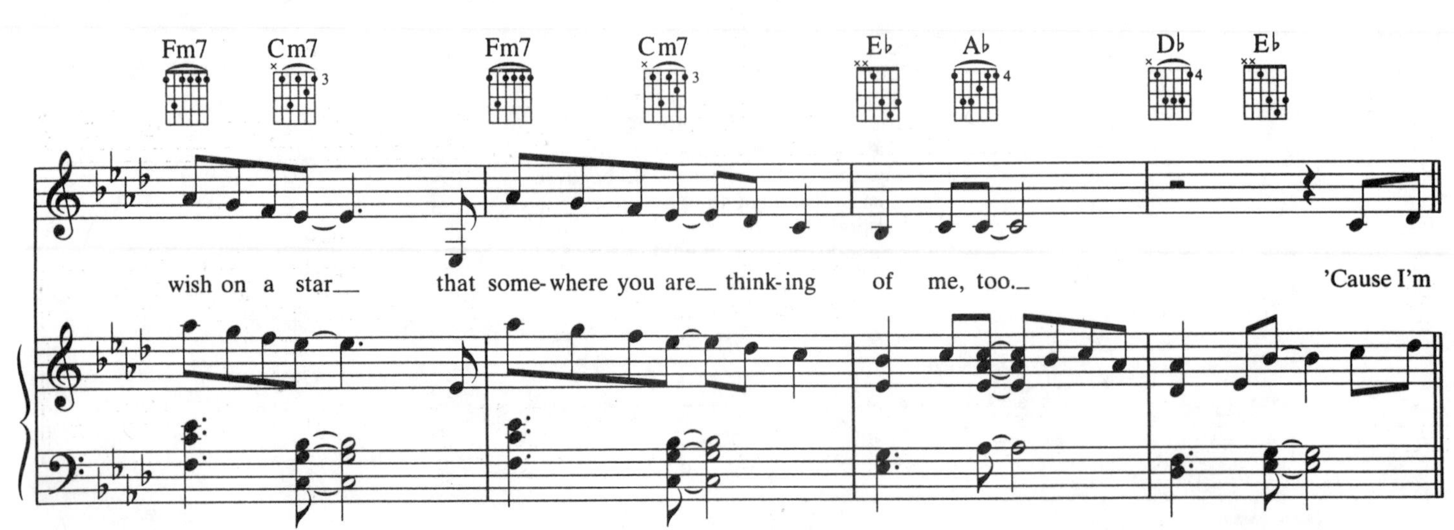

Chorus:
A♭maj7/C
D♭(9)
E♭/G
A♭
Fm7
dream - ing of you to - night. Till to - mor - row, I'll be

Gm7(♭5)
A♭maj7
Fm
B♭/F
E♭/F
A♭/C
D♭(9)
hold - ing you tight. And there's no - where in the world I'd rath - er be than

B♭m7
A♭/C
D♭
E♭7sus
A♭maj7
G♭ma7/A♭
here in my room, dream - ing a - bout you and me.

Verse:
A♭maj7
D♭maj7
G♭maj7
D♭/F
E♭/G
A♭maj7
D♭maj7
G♭maj7
2. Won-der if you ev - er see me and I won-der if you know I'm there.
3. I just wan-na hold you close but so far, all I have are dreams of you.
A♭
Fm7
Cm7
Fm7
Cm7
If you looked in my eyes, would you see what's in - side? Would you
So, I wait for the day and the cour-age to say how much
E♭/G
A♭
1.
D♭/F
E♭
2.
D♭/F
E♭
e - ven care?
I love you.
Yes, I do. I'll be

Chorus:
A♭maj7/C D♭(9) E♭/G A♭ Fm7
dream - ing of you to - night. Till to - mor - row, I'll be
Gm7(♭5) A♭maj7 Fm B♭/F E♭/F A♭/C D♭(9)
hold - ing you tight. And there's no - where in the world I'd rath - er be than
B♭m7 A♭/C D♭ E♭7sus A♭
here in my room, dream - ing a - bout you and me.
E♭m9 G♭maj7 A♭ E♭m9
Hah.
Spoken: Corazón,
I can't stop

D♭/F E♭/G A♭ E♭m9 G♭maj7 A♭
dream - ing of you. I can't stop dream - ing.
no puedo dejar de pensar en tí... stop dreaming... Como te necesito
E♭m9 D♭/F E♭/G A♭ N.C.
I can't stop dream - ing of you.
stop dreaming of you. Mi amor, como te extraño!
Verse:
B♭maj9 Cm7/B♭ B♭maj9 Cm7/B♭
4. Late at night when all the world is sleep - ing, I stay up and think of you.
B♭ Gm7 Dm7 Gm7 Dm7
And I still can't be - lieve that you came up to me and said,

F/A
B♭
E♭/G
F
"I love you."
I love you, too.
Now, I'm
Chorus:
B♭maj7/D
E♭(9)
F/A
B♭
Gm7
dream - ing with you to - night, till to - mor - row, and for
Am7(♭5)
B♭maj7
Gm
C/E
F
B♭/D
all of my life. And there's no - where in the world I'd rath - er
E♭(9)
Cm7
B♭/D
E♭
F7sus
Repeat ad lib. and fade
be than here in my room, dream-ing with you, end - less - ly

From the CBS Television Series "AS THE WORLD TURNS"

EVERY BEAT OF MY HEART

Words and Music by
BRIAN McKNIGHT and EARL ROSE

Am7
Dm7
Gm7
C7sus
C7
F(9)
been wait - ing for, hey. Close your eyes I don't care
Dm7
C/D
Gm7
Cm7
F13
B♭maj7
what oth - er peo - ple say. Here un - der-neath the stars now
B♭m7
E♭13
Am7
Dm7
Gm7
B♭/C
Ju - pi - ter and Mars don't seem so far a - way. I want you to know
mf
Chorus:
B♭maj7
C/D
Dm7
E♭/F
F13
you take my breath a - way and it's been that way right from the start.

B♭6/9
B♭maj7
E13(♭9)
E7(♯5)
E7
G/A
Am7
A♭/B♭
B♭7
I did-n't know how to tell you that I want to love
E♭6/9
Gm9
Gm11
F/G
you with ev-'ry beat of my heart, with ev-'ry beat of my heart.
Verse 2:
C7sus
F(9)
Dm7
C/D
Take my hand. Don't be a-fraid, don't go I want you
mp
Gm7
Cm7
F13
B♭maj7
to stay. Just re-lax your mind I prom-

Bbm7
Eb13
Am7
Dm7
Gm7
Bb/C
-ise that__ to-mor-row will be__ just like to-day.__ I want you to know__
Chorus:
Bbmaj7
C/D
Dm7
Eb/F
F13
__ you take my breath__ a-way__ and it's been__ that way right__ from the
Bb6/9
Bbmaj7
E13(b9)
E7(#5)
E7
G/A
Am7
Ab/Bb
Bb7
start.__ I did-n't know how to tell you that I want to love
Eb6/9
Gm9
Gm11
Csus
you with ev-'ry beat of my heart,__ with ev-'ry beat of my heart.__

F
C
C/B♭
F/A
Dm7
G
B♭13(♯11)
Am7
A13(♯9)
A7(♯5)
Dm7
B♭maj7
C/D
Dm7
I said I want you to know you take my breath a - way, and it's been
E♭/F
F13
B♭6/9
B♭maj7
E13(♭9)
E7(♯5)
E7
G/A
Am7
that way right from the start. I did-n't know how to tell you that

1.
A♭/B♭
B♭7
E♭6/9
Gm9
C11
I want to love you with ev-'ry beat of my heart.
I said I want you to know
2.
E♭
Gm7
C7sus
you with ev-'ry beat of my heart, with ev-'ry beat of my heart,
C7
F
Dm7
Gm7
with ev-'ry beat of my heart.
B♭/C
C7
B♭/C
F
With ev-'ry beat of my heart.
poco rit.
mp
pp

FOR THE FIRST TIME

Words and Music by
JAMES NEWTON HOWARD,
ALLAN RICH and JUD FRIEDMAN

Slowly 𝅗𝅥 = 62

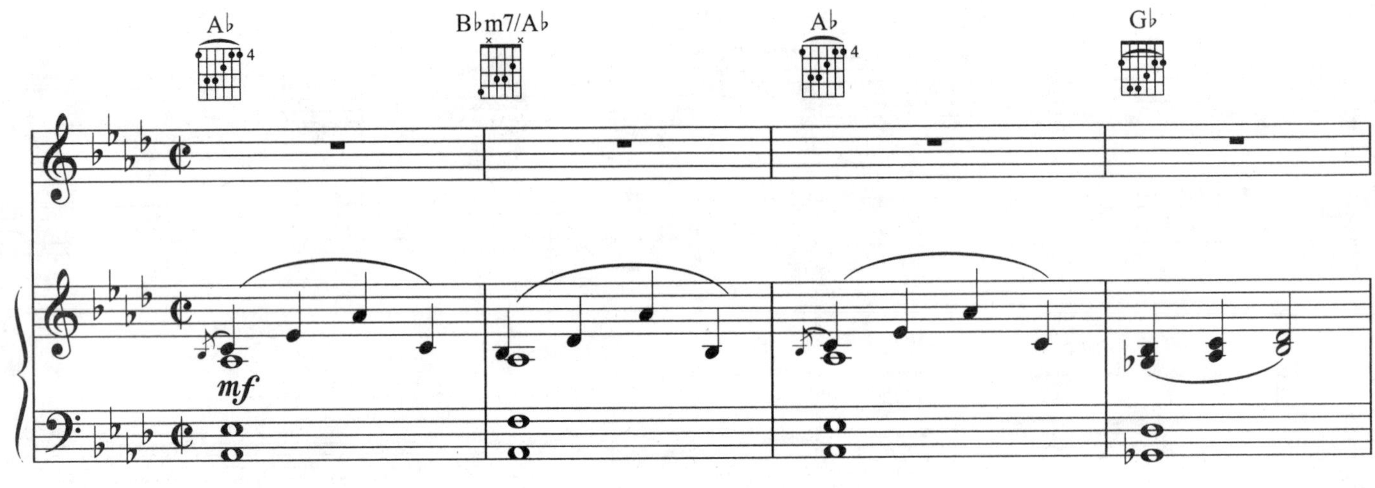

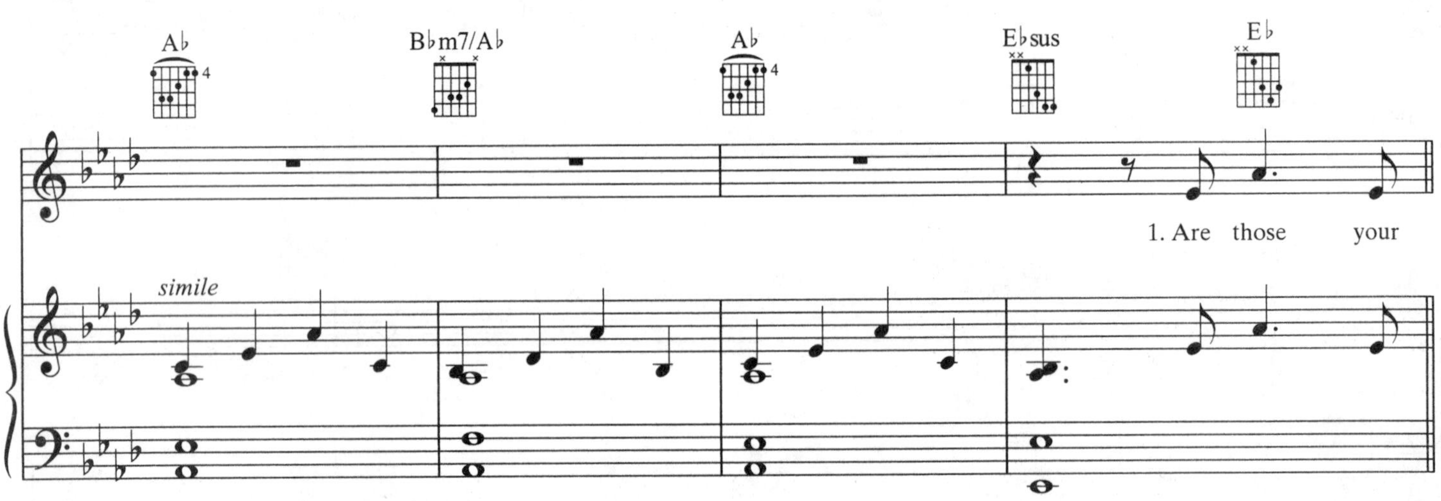

Verse:

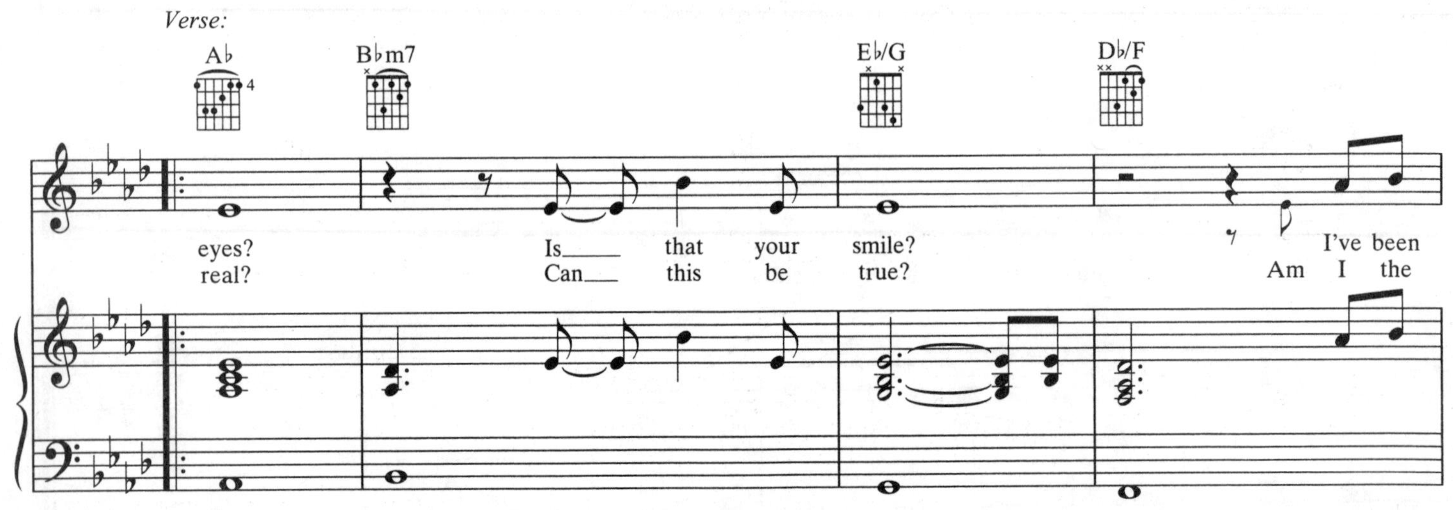

A♭
Fm7
B♭m7
E♭sus
E♭
look-ing at you for-ev - er, yet I nev - er saw you be-fore.___ Are these your
per-son I was this morn - ing, and are you the same___ you?___ It's all so
A♭
D♭/F
A♭/C
D♭
hands hold - ing mine? Now I
strange. How can it be? All a -
Fm
D♭
E♭sus
E♭
won - der how___ I could-'ve been___ so blind.
long, this love___ was right in front___ of me.
And for the
Chorus:
A♭
D♭maj9
Fm7
E♭/G
first time, I am look - ing in___ your eyes.___ For the

A♭
D♭
E♭sus
E♭
first time, I'm seeing who you are. I can't believe
D♭/F
D♭m/F♭
A♭/E♭
D♭
D♭m6
how much I see when you're looking back at me. Now I
A♭/E♭
Fm7
B♭m7
E♭sus
E♭
understand what love is, love is for the
A♭
Fm7
D♭maj9
1.
E♭sus
E♭
first time.
2. Can this be

2.
Bridge:
Ebsus
Eb
Bbm7
Fm7
Bbm7
Such a long time ago, I had given up on
Ebsus
Eb
Ab
Eb/G
Fm7
finding this emotion ever again.
Eb/G
Ab
Dm7(b5)
G7(#5 b9)
But you're here with me now, yes, I found you somehow,
G7(#5)
Cm7
Fsus
and I've never been so sure.

F
B♭
Cm7/B♭
B♭
a tempo
Chorus:
A♭
B♭
E♭maj9
Gm7
And for the first time, I am look-ing in your eyes.
F/A
B♭
E♭
Fsus
For the first time, I'm see-ing who you are.
F
E♭/G
E♭m/G♭
B♭/F
I can't be-lieve how much I see when you're look-ing back at me.

E♭
E♭m6
B♭/F
Gm7
Now I un - der - stand what love is,
Cm7
F7sus
B♭
Gm7
freely
love is for the first time.
a tempo
E♭maj9
F7sus
B♭
rit.

FOR YOU I WILL

Words and Music by
DIANE WARREN

Cm7
Cm7/F
B♭
F/A
I will be there.
An - y time the times get too tough, an - y time your
won't let you down.
If there is a moun - tain to move, I will move that
Gm7
F/G
Gm7
Cm7
Dm7
best ain't e - nough,
I'll be the one to make it bet - ter.
moun - tain for you.
I'm here for you, I'm here for - ev - er.
A♭maj7
Gm7
Cm7
I'll be there to pro - tect you,
see you through.
I will be a for - tress,
tall and strong.
I'll
E♭m7
Cm7
Cm7/F
I'll be there, and there is noth - ing I won't do.
keep you safe, I'll stand be - side you, right or wrong.
I will cross the

Chorus:
B♭
F/A
Gm7
Dm7
Cm7
Cm7/F
o-cean for you, I will go and bring you the moon, I will be your he-ro, your strength, an-y-thing
you need. I will be the sun in your sky, I will light your way for all time, prom-ise you,
To Coda
1.
Eb♭m7
E♭/F
for you, I will.
2. I will shield your
2.
Bridge:
A♭maj7
E♭/G
For you, I will lay my life on the line.

D7/F♯
Gm7
For you, I'll fight, for you, I will die. With ev-
Cm7
B♭/D
D7/F♯
Gm7
- ery breath, with all my soul, I give my word, I'll give it all.
E♭m7
Cm7/F
D.S. 𝄋 al Coda
Put your faith in me, I'll do an - y - thing. I will cross the
Coda
B♭
F/A
Cm7/F
Dm7/G
I will, I will, I will.
I will cross the

Chorus:
C
G/B
Am7
Em7
Dm7
Dm7/G
o - cean for you, I will go and bring you the moon, I will be your he - ro, your strength, an - y - thing
you need. I will be the sun in your sky, I will light your way for all time, prom - ise you,
for you, I will. Prom - ise you, for you, I will.
I prom - ise you, for you, I will.
Freely
rit.

FOREVER'S AS FAR AS I'LL GO

Words and Music by
MIKE REID

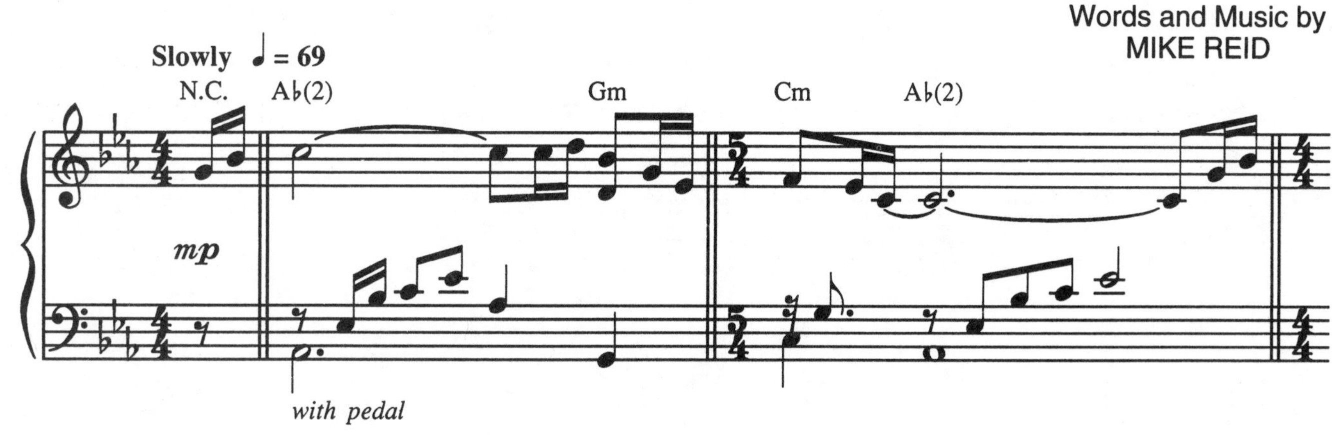

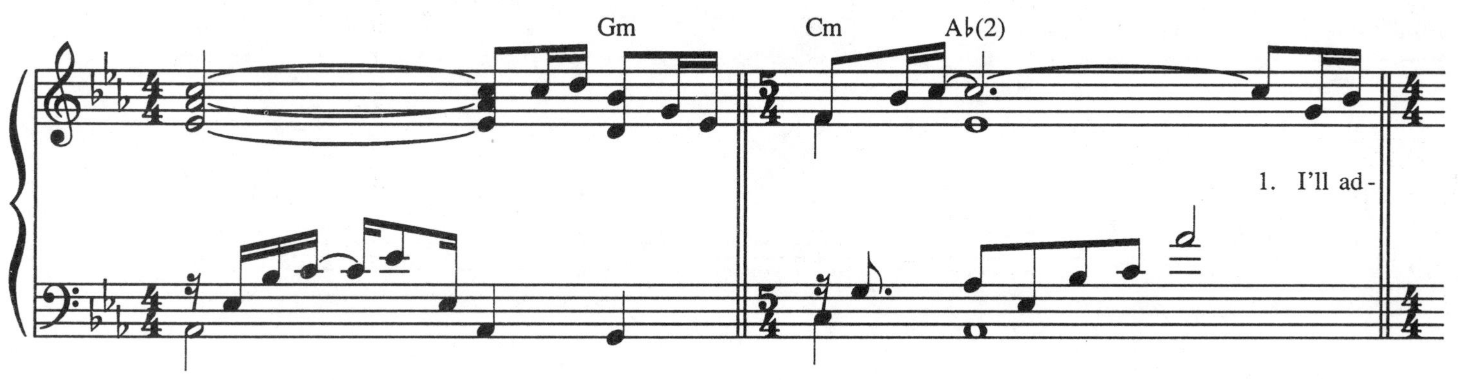

Ab6
Ab
Abmaj7/Bb
Bb
Ab/Bb
Bb
Eb/G
It's best that you know where you stand with me. I will
cresc.
mf

Chorus:
Ab
Eb
Eb(2)/G
Ab
give you my heart faith - ful and true, and all the love it can hold

Gm
Gm7
Cm7
Gm7
Ab(2) Ab
that's all I can do. But I've thought a - bout how long I'll love you,

Eb/Bb
Fm(11)
Eb/G
Ab(2)
Ab/Bb
and it's on - ly fair that you know, for - ev - er's as far as I'll

Verse 2:
When there's age around my eyes and gray in your hair,
And it only takes a touch to recall the love we've shared.
I won't take for granted that you know my love is true.
Each night in your arms, I will whisper to you...
(To Chorus:)

FROM HERE TO ETERNITY
Words and Music by
MICHAEL PETERSON and
ROBERT ELLIS ORRALL
Slowly ♩ = 79
Gsus2 sus4
G
C/G
C(9)
mf
1. I did
Verse:
G(9)
Bm7
C
D
ev - 'ry - thing_ I could_ to get you here_ to-night with-out tell-ing you why._
2. See additional lyrics
Am7
Now, girl, if you on - ly would,_ please hold out your hand___
and just close_ your eyes.___ I've been dy - ing to ask you
Dsus
one burn-ing ques-tion: Will_ you be mine?___ From here to___ e -
From Here to Eternity - 3 - 1

Chorus:

G Bm7 C D G Bm7

ter - ni - ty, I'm ask - ing you to___ share your life___ with me.___ Now___

C D Em7 Bm7 C *To Coda* ⊕

___ and for - ev - er, I guar - an - tee___ I'll___ al - ways stay___ by your side.___

Dsus G Bm7 C D

___ I prom - ise___ my love to you, I'm will - ing and a - ble and read -

G Bm7 C D Em7 Bm7

y to...___ what - ev - er you need,___ I am here___ for you.___ And

Am7 G/B C D Gsus2 sus4 G

I'll al - ways be,___ from here to e - ter - ni - ty.

Verse 2:
Well, I saved a year for this ring,
I can't wait to see how it looks on your hand.
I'll give you everything that one woman needs
From a one-woman man.
I'll be strong, I'll be tender, a man of my word.
And I will be yours...
(To Chorus:)

FROM THIS MOMENT ON

D/F♯
D/G
G
for better, for worse, I will love you with ev - 'ry beat of my heart.
C
D
G/C
1. From this
Slowly ♩ = 72
Verse 1:
G5
C (9)
mo - ment life has be - gun. From this mo - ment
D5
C (9)
G5
you are the one. Right be - side you is where I be - long,

Am
D
G5
Verse 2:
from this mo - ment on.
2. From this mo - ment I have been blessed.
C (9)
D5
I live on - ly for your hap - pi - ness. And for your
C (9)
G5
Am
D
love I'd give my last breath, from this mo - ment on.
Chorus:
C (9)
G
C (9)
I give my hand to you with all my heart. Can't

D
G
wait to live my life with you, can't wait to start.
You and I will nev - er be a -
C(9)
Em7
C(9)
part.
My dreams
came true
be - cause
G
G/D
D
N.C.
Verse 3:
A(9)
E
of you.
3. From this
mo - ment,
as long as I live,
D
E
I will
love you,
I prom - ise you this.
There is noth-

D
A
Bm
E
ing I would - n't give,
from this mo - ment on.
D(9)
A
F♯m7
D(9)
E
Chorus:
A
You're the rea - son I be - lieve in
D
E
love.
And you're the an - swer to my prayers from

A
up a - bove.
All we need is just the two of
D
F♯m7
D(9)
us.
My dreams
came true
be - cause
A
A/E
E
N.C.
of you.
4. From this
Verse 4:
B
mo - ment,
as long as I live,
I will

E
F♯
E
love you, I promise you this. There is nothing I would-n't give,
B
C♯m
F♯
E(9)
from this mo-ment. I will love you, I will love you as
B
C♯m
E
long as I live, from this mo - ment
E(9)
B/D♯
F♯7
B
on.
on.
Mm, mm.
rit.

From the Original Motion Picture Soundtrack "DON JUAN DeMARCO"

HAVE YOU EVER REALLY LOVED A WOMAN?

Lyrics by
BRYAN ADAMS and
ROBERT JOHN "MUTT" LANGE

Music by
MICHAEL KAMEN

Cm
Gm/B♭
F/A
Dsus2/4
D
Dsus2/4
D
find your-self ly - ing help - less in her arms,
see your un - born chil - dren in her eyes,
you know you real - ly
you know you real - ly
C/G
G
Chorus:
love a wom - an.
love a wom - an.
cresc.
When you love a wom-an, you tell her that she's real - ly
mf
D
want - ed.
When you love a wom - an, you tell her that she's the
G
one.
Em7
She needs some-bod - y to tell her that it's gon-na
'Cause she needs some-bod - y to tell her that you'll al-ways

Am7
D
Am7
D
Am7
D
Am7
D
last______ for-ev - er.
be______ to-geth - er.
So tell me, have you ev-er real - ly, real-ly, real-ly, ev-er loved__ a
1.
2.
G
G
wom-an?______
2. To real-ly love a
wom-an.______
You've got to
3
Bridge:
E♭
G
give her some faith, hold her__ tight, a lit-tle ten - der - ness. You've got to treat her__ right!

D
G
She will be there for you, tak-ing good care of you. You real-ly got-ta love your wom-an.
(Instrumental solo . . .
E♭
Cm6
D
B♭
F
2
B♭
F/A
F
And when you
. . . end solo)
Cm
Gm/B♭
F/A
Dsus2/4
D
Dsus2/4
D
find your-self ly - ing help - less in her arms, you know you real - ly
2

C/G
G
love a wom - an. When
D
Chorus:
3
you love a wom-an, you tell her that she's real-ly want-ed. When
mf
G
you love a wom - an, you tell her that she's the one.
Em7
Am7
D
Am7
D
She needs some-bod - y to tell her that it's gon-na last for-ev - er. So

Am7 D Am7 D G

tell me, have you ev-er real - ly, real-ly, real-ly ev-er loved__ a wom-an?______ So

Am7 D Am7 D G

tell me, have you ev-er real - ly, real-ly, real-ly ev-er loved__ a wom-an? Oh, just

Freely

Am7 D Am7 D

tell me, have you ev - er real - ly, real - ly, real - ly ev - er loved______ a

G

wom - an?____

p

From the Touchstone Motion Picture "CON AIR"

HOW DO I LIVE

Words and Music by
DIANE WARREN

F♯m7
G♯m7
C♯m7
Em7/A
ba- by, you would take a- way__ ev - 'ry- thing__
good in my life.___
And tell me
𝄋 Chorus:
D
A
G
F♯m7
now, how do I live with - out___
you? I want to know.
How do I breathe with - out__
Bm7
Em7
G(9)
__ you, if you ev - er go?__
How do I ev - er,
ev - er sur - vive?_
To Coda
1.
F♯m7/B
__ How do I,
how do I,
oh, how do I
live?
2. With - out you,_
2.
F♯m
Em7
how do I,
oh, how do I
live?

Bm7
F♯m7
F♯m7/B
If
G♯m7
C♯m7
F♯m7
you ev - er leave,
ba - by, you would take a - way ev - 'ry - thing.
G♯m7
C♯m7
F♯m7
Need you with me.
Ba - by, 'coz you know that you're ev - - 'ry - thing
G♯m7
C♯m7
Em7/A
D.S. 𝄋 al Coda
good in my life.
And tell me

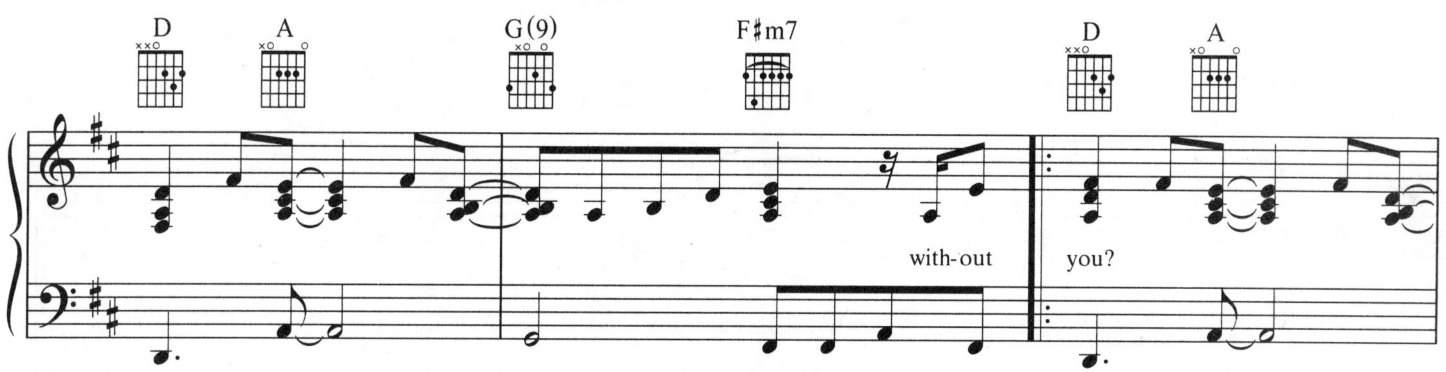

Repeat ad lib. and fade
(vocal 1st time only)

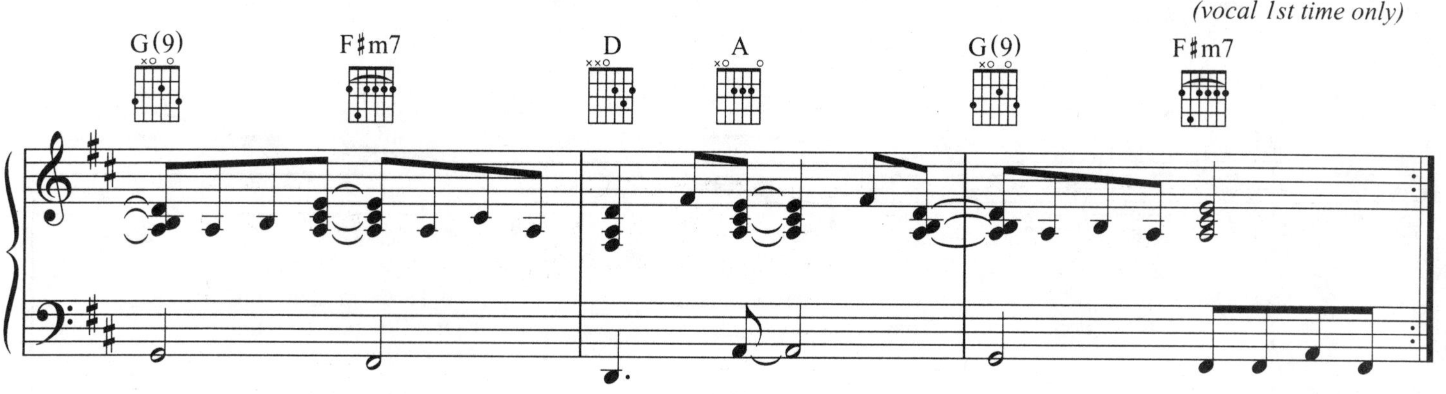

Verse 2:
Without you, there'd be no sun in my sky,
There would be no love in my life,
There'd be no world left for me.
And I, baby, I don't know what I would do,
I'd be lost if I lost you.
If you ever leave,
Baby, you would take away everything real in my life.
And tell me now...
(To Chorus:)

HOW 'BOUT US

Words and Music by
DANA WALDEN

A
1.
Dm/A
and if the fi - re's out we should both be gone.
too man - y lov - er's hearts
G9
Both:
To Next Strain
2.
Dm/A
Oh.
lose their dream. (We won't lose it!)
cresc.
Chorus:
A
Both:
D/A
Some peo-ple are made for each oth - er;
some peo-ple can love one an-oth-er for life;
Dm/A
A
how 'bout us?

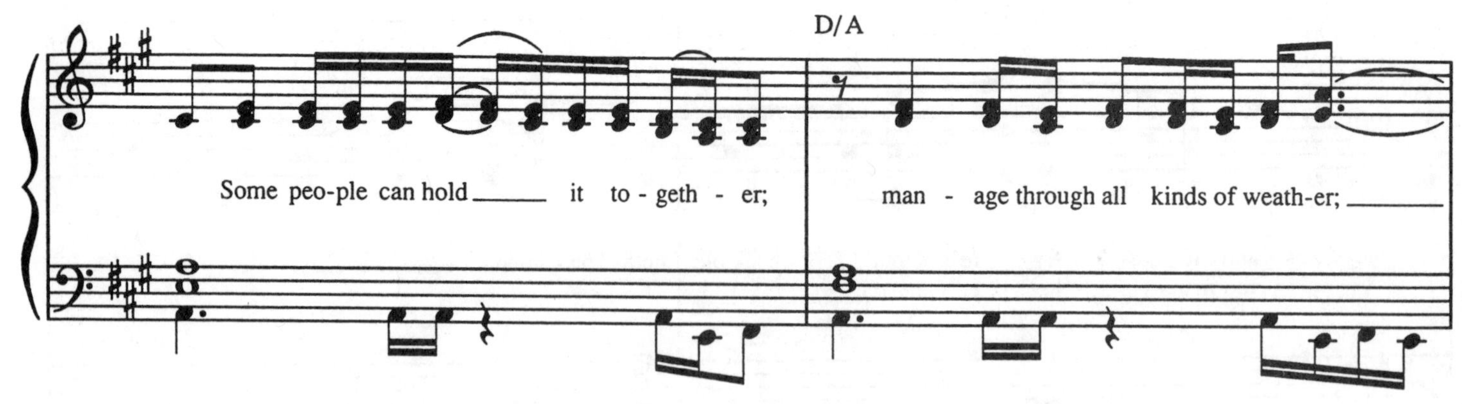
D/A
Some peo-ple can hold it to-geth - er;
man - age through all kinds of weath-er;

Dm/A
1.
A
Dm/A
Dm6/A
can
we?

A
Dm/A
D.S.
2.
A
we? How 'bout us? How 'bout us, ba-by?
dim.

Dm6/A
A
How 'bout us? How 'bout us, ba - by?
How 'bout us? How 'bout us, ba - by?

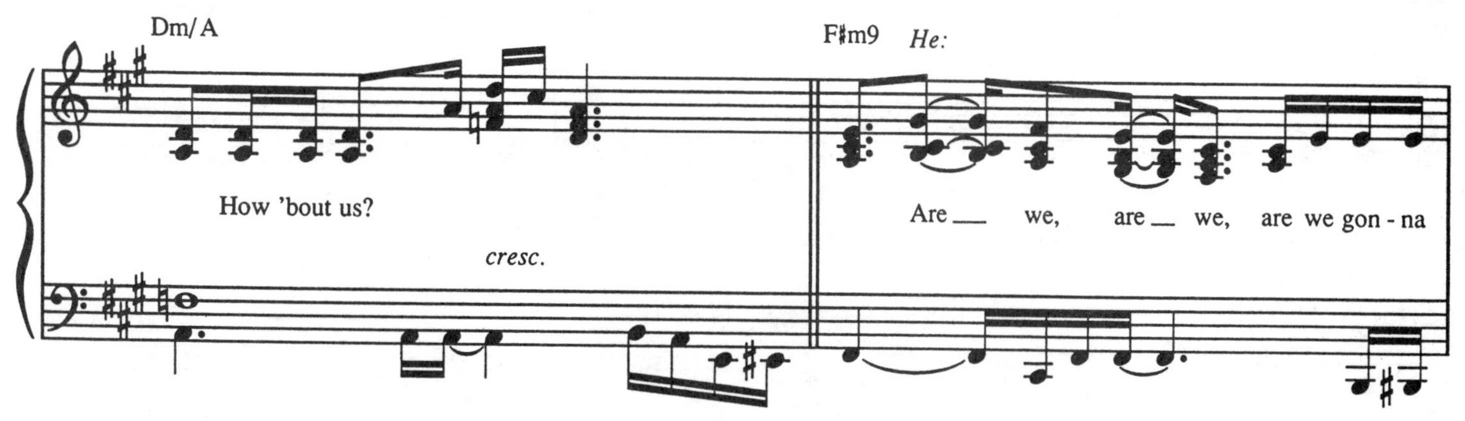
Dm/A
F♯m9
He:
How 'bout us?
cresc.
Are we, are we, are we gon-na

C♯m11
She:
He:
Both:
Em9
make it girl? I hope we can. Are we gon-na
drift, and drift, and drift, and drift, and

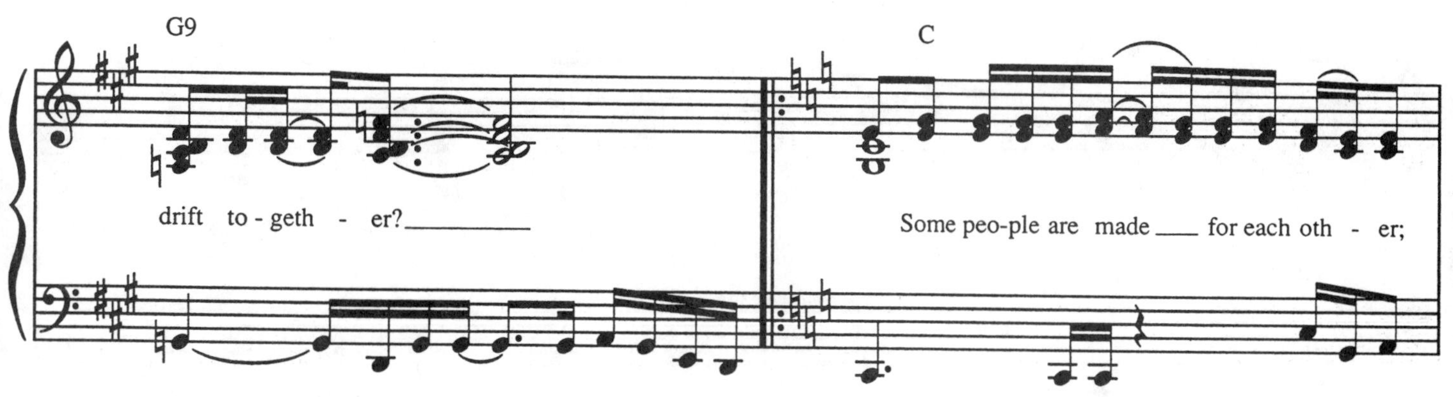
G9
C
drift to-geth - er?
Some peo-ple are made for each oth - er;

F/C
Fm/C
some peo-ple can love one an-oth-er for life;
how 'bout

C
us?
Some peo-ple can hold it to-geth - er;

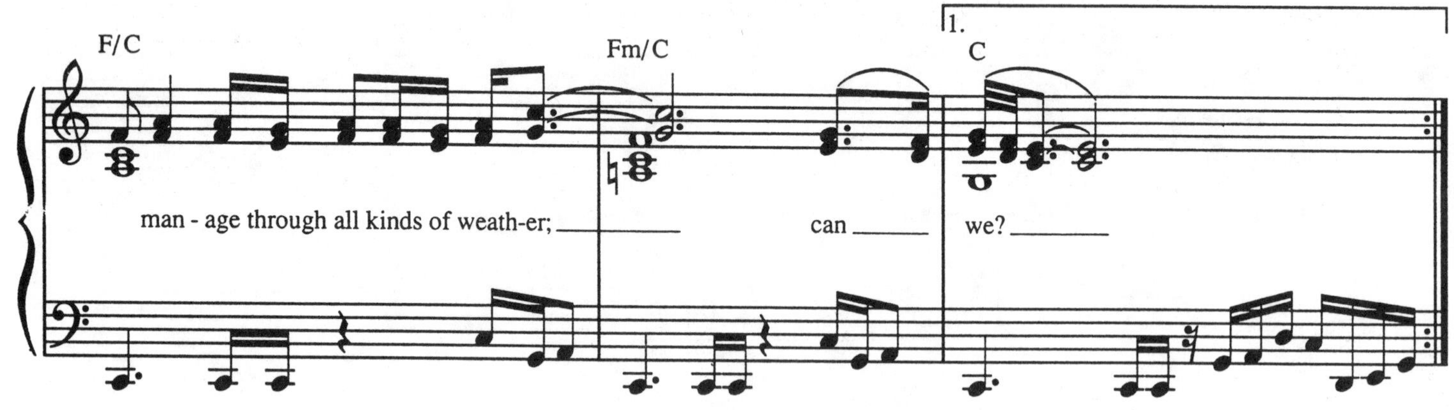
F/C
Fm/C
1.
C
man - age through all kinds of weath-er;
can
we?

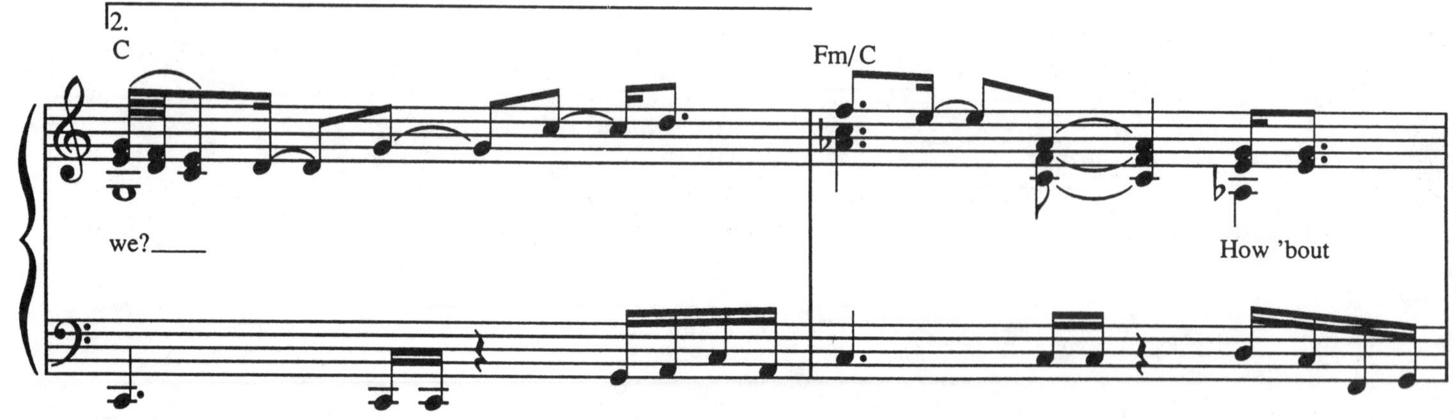
2.
C
Fm/C
we?
How 'bout

C
Fm/C
Repeat ad lib. and fade
us?
How 'bout

I CAN LOVE YOU LIKE THAT

Words and Music by
STEVE DIAMOND, MARIBETH DERRY
and JENNIFER KIMBALL

Verse:
E♭
E♭/G
A♭(9)
read you Cin-der-el-la, you hoped it would come true;_ that one day your Prince Charm-ing would come
nev-er make a prom-ise I don't in-tend to keep,_ so when I say for-ev-er, for-
Fm7/B♭
E♭
E♭/G
res-cue you._____ You like ro-man-tic mov-ies, and you nev-er will for-get the
ev-er's what I mean. I'm no Ca-sa-no-va, but I swear this much is true:
A♭(9)
Fm7/B♭
Gm7
way you felt when Ro-me-o kissed Ju-li-et._____ And all this time that you've been_ wait-
I'll be hold-ing noth-ing back when it comes to you._____ You dream of love that's ev-er-last-
A♭(9)
Gm7
A♭(9)
-ing. You don't have to wait no_ more._____ I can love you like that,_
-ing, ba-by, op-en up your_ eyes._____

Chorus:
E♭
E♭/G
A♭(9)
I would make you my world, move heav-en and earth if you were my girl.
Fm7/B♭
E♭
E♭/G
I will give you my heart, be all that you need, show you you're ev -
A♭(9)
E♭/G
Fm7
E♭
D♭maj9
Cm7
Fm7/B♭
- ery-thing that's pre-cious to me. If you give me a chance,
1.
E♭
Cm7
3
I can love you like that. I can love you like that.
I'll love you like that.

Dbmaj9
Fm7/Bb
2. Eb
2. I
I'll love you like that.
Bridge:
Bbm7
Fm7
If you want tenderness, I've got tenderness, and I
Ebsus
Eb
Ebsus
Eb
Bbm7
see through to the heart of you. If you want a man who will un-
Fm7
Ab(9)
Fm7/Bb
derstand, you don't have to look very far.

I can love you, I can love you, love you, I can love you like that,
Chorus:
E
E/G♯
A(9)
I would make you my world, move heav-en and earth if you were my girl.
F♯m7/B
E
I will give you my heart, be all that you need,
E/G♯
A(9)
Repeat ad lib. and fade
F♯m7
show you you're ev - ery-thing that's pre-cious to me. If you give me a chance,

From the Original Soundtrack Album "THE PREACHER'S WIFE"

I BELIEVE IN YOU AND ME

Words and Music by
SANDY LINZER and DAVID WOLFERT

B
Bmaj7
D♯m7/G♯
G♯m7
D♯m7
you will al-ways be the one for me. Oh, yes, you will.
C♯m7 C♯m7/F♯
B
B/A
And I be-lieve in dreams a-gain. I be-lieve that love will nev-er end. And
E(9)/G♯
Em7
A9
B/F♯
like the riv-er finds the sea, I was lost, now I'm
D♯m7
G♯m7
C♯m7
C♯m7/F♯
1.
B
C♯m7/F♯
N.C.
free, 'cause I be-lieve in you and me. 2. I will nev-er leave

2.
Bridge:
B
D♯m7
G♯m7
D♯m7
G♯m7
me.
May-be I'm a fool
to feel the way I do.
mf
C♯m7
C♯m(maj7)
C♯m7
C♯m7/F♯
N.C.
Dm7/G
I would play the fool for-ev-er just to be with you for-ev-er.
3. I be-lieve in
Verse:
C
C/B♭
Fmaj9
mir-a-cles,
and love's
a mir-a-cle.
And yes, ba-by, you're my dream come true.
Fm7/B♭
A♭/B♭
B♭/A♭
Fmaj7
C/G
Em7
Am7
I was lost,
now I'm free,
oh ba-by, 'cause

Verse 2:
I will never leave your side,
I will never hurt your pride.
When all the chips are down,
I will always be around,
Just to be right where you are, my love.
Oh, I love you, boy.
I will never leave you out,
I will always let you in
To places no one has ever been.
Deep inside, can't you see?
I believe in you and me.
(To Bridge:)

I COULD NOT ASK FOR MORE

Words and Music by
DIANE WARREN

Moderately slow rock ♩ = 66
Guitar capo 3
D
Gmaj7
D
Piano
F
B♭maj7
F
mf
Gmaj7
B♭maj7
Verse:
D
F
Gmaj7
B♭maj7
1. Lay-ing here with you, lis-t'ning to the rain,
2. Look-ing in your eyes, see-ing all I need,
D
F
Gmaj7
B♭maj7
smil-ing just to see the smile up-on your face.
ev-'ry-thing you are is ev-'ry-thing to me.

F♯m7 Am7 — G B♭ — G/A B♭/C

(1.3.) These are the mo - ments___ I thank God that I'm___ a - live.___
(2.) These are the mo - ments___ I know heav - en must_ ex - ist.___

F♯m7 Am7 — Bm7 Dm7 — E7 G7

These are the mo - ments___ I'll re - mem - ber all___ my life.___
These are the mo - ments___ I know all I need_ is this.___
(1.) I found
(2.) I have
(3.) I've got

Em7 Gm7 — G B♭ — G/A B♭/C — 1. D F

all I've wait - ed for___ and I could not ask for more._

Gmaj7 B♭maj7 — 2.3. Dsus Fsus

___ I could not ask for

cresc.

Chorus:
Gmaj7
B♭maj7
D
F
more than this time to - geth - er. I could not ask for more than this time with you. Ev - 'ry
f
C
E♭
G/B
B♭/D
Asus
Csus
prayer I have's been an - swered and ev - 'ry dream I have's come true. And
G2
B♭2
D
F
Dm/F
Fm/A♭
Dm
Fm
To Coda
right here in this mo-ment is right where I'm meant to be. Oh, here with you, here with
Asus
Csus
A
C
Asus
Csus
A
C
D
F
me, oh.
dim.
mf

Gmaj7
D
Gmaj7
D.S.𝄋 al Coda
B♭maj7
F
B♭maj7
Coda
A sus
Csus
G2
B♭2
me.
I could not ask for
more_ than the love you give_ me,
'coz it's
D/F♯
Em7
Em7/A
D
F/A
Gm7
Gm7/C
F
all I've wait-ed for
and I could not ask for more,
oh,
dim.
mf
G2
D
Gmaj7
Repeat ad lib. and fade
B♭2
F
B♭maj7
ah,
oh
yeah.
And I could not ask for more..

I CROSS MY HEART

Words and Music by
STEVE DORFF and ERIC KAZ

Fm7
E♭/G
A♭
4fr.
From here on af - ter let's stay the way we are right now.
B♭
Fm7
E♭/G
And share all the love and laugh - ter that a
D♭
4fr.
B♭7sus4
B♭7
3
life - time will al - low.
E♭
E♭/G
A♭
4fr.
B♭
f
I cross my heart and prom - ise to

E♭
E♭/G
A♭
4fr.
give all I've got to give to make all
A♭/B♭
4fr.
B♭7
E♭
E♭/G
your dreams come true.
In all the
A♭
4fr.
B♭
B♭/A♭
E♭/G
A♭
4fr.
E♭/G
world you'll nev - er find a love as
Fm7
B♭7
To Coda
1.
E♭
true as mine.
mp

A♭
E♭/G
Fm7
B♭7
E♭
You will
2. E♭
A♭
E♭/G
mine.
And if a - long the way we find a day
Fm7
B♭7
E♭
G♭
it starts to storm.
You've got the prom - ise of my love
D♭/F
E♭m7
G♭/A♭
A♭/B♭
D.S. al Coda
to keep you warm.

Additional Lyrics

2. You will always be the miracle
That makes my life complete.
And as long as there's a breath in me
I'll make yours just as sweet.
As we look into the future,
It's as far as we can see.
So let's make each tomorrow
Be the best that it can be.
(To Chorus)

I DO (CHERISH YOU)

Words and Music by
KEITH STEGALL and DAN HILL

*Enharmonic chord labeling of F♭maj7.

B♭m11
A♭(9)/C
E♭11
When you smile, I can feel all my pas-sion un-fold-ing.
D♭(9)
A♭(9)/C
D♭(9)
Your hand brush-es mine, and a thou-sand sen-sa-tions se-
Chorus:
E♭11
A♭(9)
Fm9
duce me, 'cause I... I do cher-ish you, for the
cresc.
mf
B♭m11
E♭11
A♭(9)
rest of my life. You don't have to think twice; I will love you still.

Fm9
B♭m11
C7sus
C7
From the depths of my soul, it's be - yond my con - trol. I've wait - ed so
Fm
Fm/E♭
Dm7(♭5)
B♭m7
long to say this to you. If you're ask - ing do I love you this much,
1.
E♭7sus
A♭(9)
Fm9
I do. Oh, ba - by.
dim.
mp
B♭m11
C♭
G♭/B♭
D♭(9)/F
2.
E♭7sus
2. In my world yes, I
cresc.

Bmaj7
B7
B♭m7
A7(♯5)
do.
If you're
A♭m7
B♭m11
E♭/F
ask - ing do I love you this much,
ba - by, I do
cresc.
B♭(9)
Gm9
Cm7
cher - ish you.
From the depths of my soul, it's be -
f
D7sus
D7(♯5)
Gm
Gm/F
Em7(♭5)
yond my con - trol. I've wait - ed so long to say this to you.
If you're
dim. poco a poco

Cm7
F7sus
F11
ask - ing do I love you this much,___
well, ba - by, I do.___
B♭(9)
Gm9
E♭6/9
B♭/F
F7
B♭(9)
Ah,___
I___ do.
rit. e dim.

Verse 2:
In my world before you,
I lived outside my emotions.
Didn't know where I was going
Till that day I found you.
How you opened my life
To a new paradise.
In a world torn by change,
Still with all of my heart,
Till my dying day . . .
(To Chorus:)

I DO

Words and Music by
PAUL BRANDT

Verses 2 & 3:

C F G Gsus G C F
E♭ A♭ B♭ B♭sus B♭ E♭ A♭

mp 2. I know the ques-tions in your___ mind,__ but go a-head and ask me one more__
3. See additional lyrics

G Am G/B C Fmaj7
B♭ Cm B♭/D E♭ A♭maj7

__ time. You'll find the an - swer's still__ the

G Em F(9) G
B♭ Gm A♭(9) B♭

same, it won't change from day_ to day___ for worse_ or___ bet - ter. Will I

Chorus:

C G7/B Am G F G C G7/B Am G
E♭ B♭7/D Cm B♭ A♭ B♭ E♭ B♭7/D Cm B♭

prom-ise to be___ your best friend? And____ am I here__ un - til__

mf

F G Em F C G
A♭ B♭ Gm A♭ E♭ B♭

______ the end?__ Can I be sure I have been wait - in' for you?

Em F Em F
Gm A♭ Gm A♭
And did I say my love is true? Ba-by, I
dim.
1.
C G7/B Am G F G C G/B Am G
E♭ B♭7/D Cm B♭ A♭ B♭ E♭ B♭7/D Cm B♭
will, I am, I can, I have, I do.
F(9)
A♭(9)
2.
C G7/B Am G F(9) G
E♭ B♭7/D Cm B♭ A♭(9) B♭
will, I am, I can, I have, I do.
mp
Fmaj7 C G
A♭maj7 E♭ B♭
mf (Instrumental solo...
3

Verse 3:
I know the time will disappear,
But this love we're building on will always be here.
No way that this is sinking sand,
On this solid rock we'll stand forever...
(To Chorus:)

(EVERYTHING I DO) I DO IT FOR YOU

From The Motion Picture "Robin Hood: Prince Of Thieves"

Written by
BRYAN ADAMS, ROBERT JOHN LANGE
and MICHAEL KAMEN

Dbsus2
Ab/Db
Gb
Db/Ab
Ab
soul, and when you find me there you'll search no more. Don't
life, I would give it all, I would sac - ri - fice. Don't
Ebm
Dbm
Ebm
Db/Eb
Ebm
Db
tell me it's not worth fight - ing for. You can't tell me it's not worth dy - ing
tell me it's not worth fight - ing for. I can't help it, there's noth - ing I want
Ebm
Db
Absus4
for. more. You know it's true, ev - 'ry - thing I do, I do it for
Db5
Db
Dbsus4
Db
you. you. There's

C♭
F♭
C♭
G♭
no love like your love, and no oth - er could give more love. There's
D♭
4fr.
A♭
E♭
A♭
Absus4
no way, un - less you're there all the time, all the way, yeah.
G♭(addA♭)
D♭
G♭(addA♭)
D♭

Ebm
Ab
Absus4
Ab
Oh, you can't tell me it's not worth try-ing for. I can't
Db
Dbsus4
help it, there's noth-ing I want more. Yeah, I would fight for you, I'd
Gb
Gbm
lie for you, walk the mile for you, yeah, I'd die for you. You know it's
a tempo
Db/Ab
Gb6
true, ev-'ry-thing I do, oh, oh, I do it for you.
rit.

From Touchstone Pictures' ARMAGEDDON

I DON'T WANT TO MISS A THING

G
D/F♯
Em7
smile while you are sleep - ing, while you're far a - way and dream - ing. I could
D
A/C♯
Bm7
G
D/F♯
spend my life in this sweet sur - ren- der. I could stay lost in this mo- ment for-
Em7
F♯m7
Gmaj7
Asus
ev - er. Ev-'ry mo- ment spent with you is a mo- ment I treas - ure.
Chorus:
D
A/C♯
Em7
Don't wan- na close my eyes, don't wan- na fall a - sleep, 'coz I'd

G
A
D
A/C♯
miss you, ba - by, and I don't wan - na miss a thing. 'Coz e - ven when I dream of you,
Em7
G
A
To Coda
the sweet - est dream would nev - er do. I'd still miss you, ba - by, and I don't wan - na miss a thing.
D
A/C♯
Bm7
2. Lay - ing
Verse 2:
D
A/C♯
Bm7
close to you, feel - ing your heart beat - ing, and I'm

G
D/F♯
Em7
won - d'ring what you're dream - ing, won-d'ring if it's me you're see - ing. Then I
D
A/C♯
Bm7
kiss your eyes_ and thank God we're to - geth - er.___ I just wan - na
F♯m7
Gmaj7
Asus
D.S. 𝄋 al Coda
stay with you___ in this mo - ment for - ev - er, for - ev - er and ev - er.___
Bridge:
Coda
D
C
___ I don't wan - na miss one smile;___ I don't wan - na

G/B
B♭
miss one kiss. I just wan-na be with you, right here with you,
F/A
C
just like this. I just wan-na hold you close, feel your heart so
G/B
Dm7
close to mine, and just stay here in this mo-ment for all the
Asus
A
rest of time. Ba-by, ba-by.

Chorus:
D
A/C♯
Em7
Don't wan-na close my eyes, don't wan-na fall a-sleep, 'coz I'd
G
A
D
A/C♯
miss you, ba-by, and I don't wan-na miss a thing. 'Coz e-ven when I dream of you,
Em7
G
A
the sweet-est dream would nev-er do. I'd still miss you, ba-by, and I don't wan-na miss a thing.
D
A/C♯
Em7
Don't wan-na close my eyes, don't wan-na fall a-sleep, 'coz I'd

G
A
Bm7
A/C♯
miss you, ba - by, and I don't wan-na miss a thing. 'Coz e - ven when I dream of you,
Em7
G
A
the sweet - est dream would nev - er do. I'd still miss you, ba - by, and I don't wan-na miss a thing.
D
A/C♯
Em7
G
A
Repeat ad lib. and fade
D
A/C♯
Em7
G
A

YOU MUST LOVE ME

Words by
TIM RICE

Music by
ANDREW LLOYD WEBBER

F11 F Bb F/Bb Bb

Cer-tain-ties dis-ap-pear

Bb7 Eb Cm7

what do we do ___ for our dream to sur-vive, how do we keep _ all our

F11 F F11 F D7

pas-sions a-live as we used to do? ___ Deep in my heart I'm con-

Gm D7 Gm D7
ceal - ing things that I'm long-ing to say, scared to con-fess what I'm

Additional Lyrics

Verse 2: *(Instrumental 8 bars)*
Why are you at my side?
How can I be any use to you now?
Give me a chance and I'll let you see how
Nothing has changed.
Deep in my heart I'm concealing
Things that I'm longing to say,
Scared to confess what I'm feeling
Frightened you'll slip away,
You must love me.

RIGHT WHERE I BELONG

Words and Music by VICTORIA SHAW,
BRYAN WHITE and EARL ROSE

Gm
F
E♭(9)
B♭/D
E♭
I was so___ a - lone.___ Now you're here___ and the mys -
that was an - oth - er time.___ So let go___ and give in___

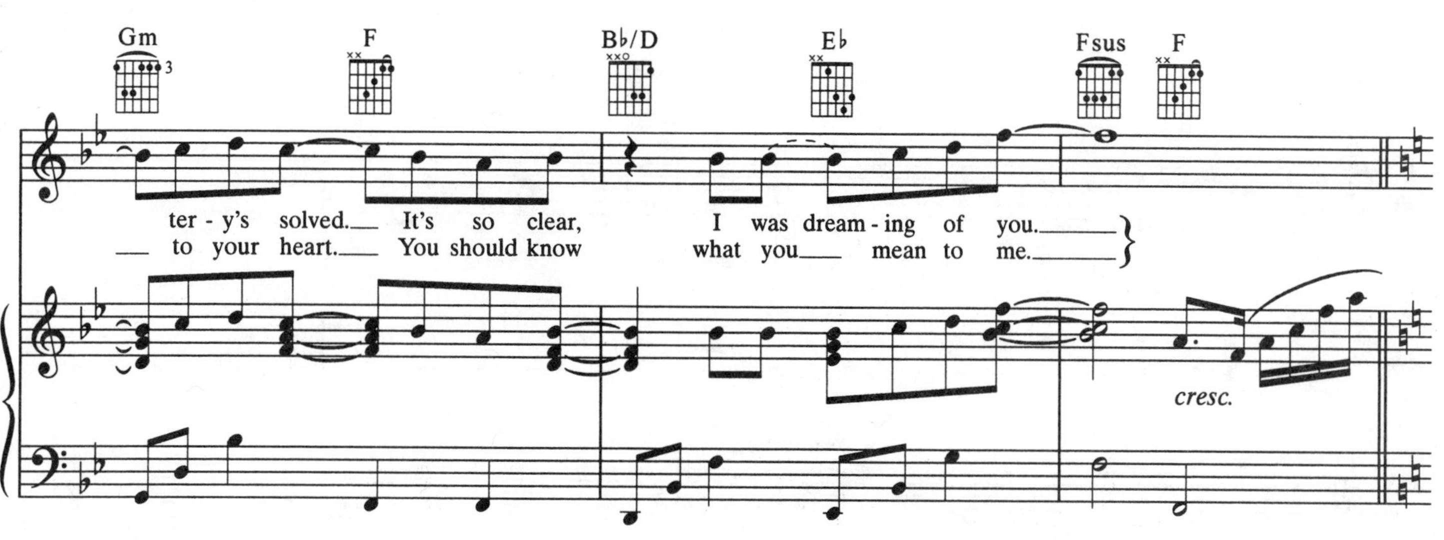
Gm
F
B♭/D
E♭
Fsus
F
ter - y's solved.___ It's so clear, I was dream - ing of you.___
___ to your heart.___ You should know what you___ mean to me.___
cresc.

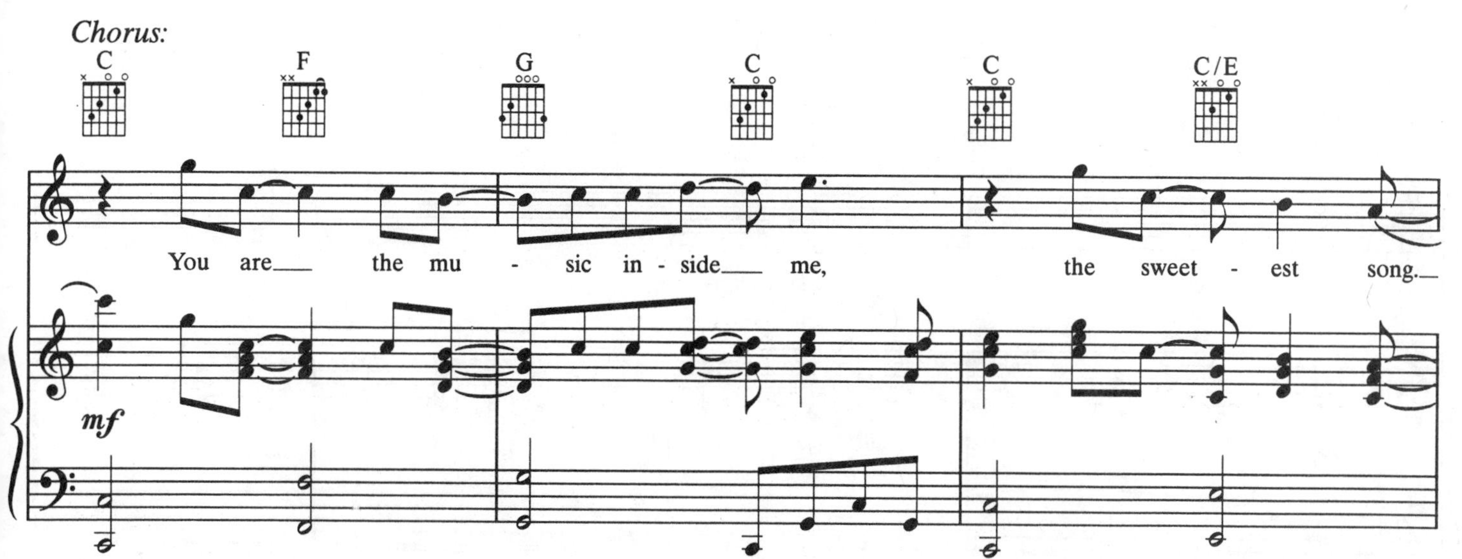
Chorus:
C
F
G
C
C
C/E
You are___ the mu - sic in - side___ me, the sweet - est song.___
mf

1.
F
C
F
G
Am
And you are the light that guides me safe -

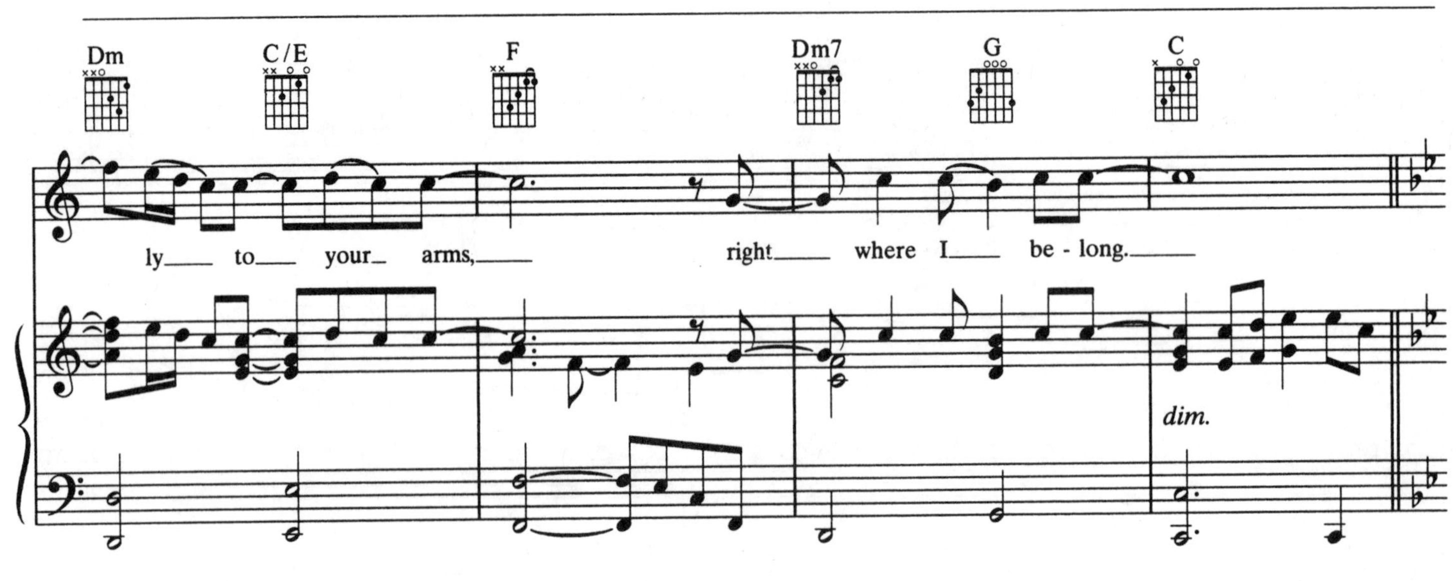
Dm
C/E
F
Dm7
G
C
ly to your arms, right where I be - long.
dim.

B♭
F/B♭
F/B♭
mp

2.
C F G Am Dm C/E
And you are the light that guides me safe - ly to your arms,
F Dm7 G C G/B
right where I be - long.
rit. e dim.
F/A G F G
Right where I be -
mp
B♭(9) F/A Gsus C
long.
a tempo
rit. e dim.
p

From the Motion Picture "THE MIRROR HAS TWO FACES"

I FINALLY FOUND SOMEONE

Words and Music by
BARBRA STREISAND, MARVIN HAMLISCH,
R.J. LANGE and BRYAN ADAMS

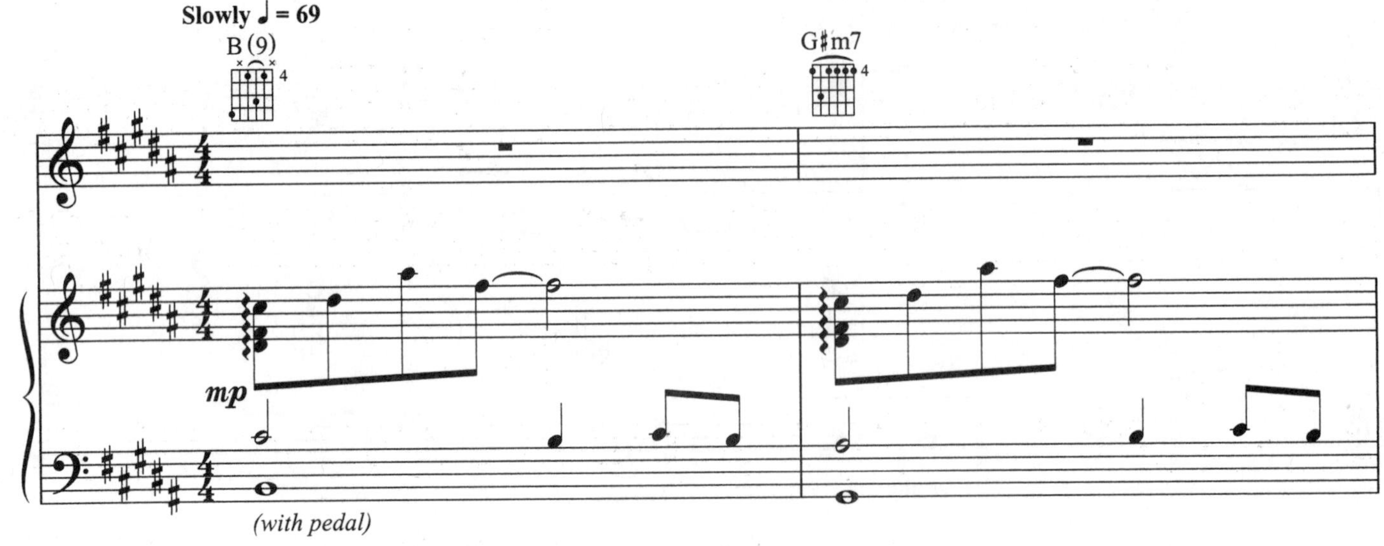

Emaj9
Em6
I fi-n'lly found the one___ that makes me feel com-plete.
B(9)
G♯m7
It start-ed o - ver cof - fee, we start-ed out as friends.
C♯m7/F♯
It's fun-ny how, from sim-ple things,_ the best things be - gin.
A♭(9)
Fm7
___ This time, it's dif-f'rent, it's all be-cause of you._

D♭maj9
D♭m6
It's bet-ter than it's ev - er been
'cause we can talk it
through.
through, yeah.
A♭(9)
Fm7
My fa-v'rite line
was, "Can I call you some - time?"
D♭maj9
D♭m6
It's all you had to say
to take my breath a - way.
Chorus:
F(9)
This is it! Oh, I fi - n'lly
mf

B♭maj9
B♭m6
F(9)
found some - one, some - one to share_ my life. I fi - n'lly
B♭maj9
B♭m6
F(9)
found the one_ to be with ev - 'ry_ night._ 'Cause what -
A7sus
A7
Dm
D♭
ev - er I do,_ it's just got to be you. My
F/C
B♭/C
life has just be - gun,_ I fi - n'lly found some - one._

F(9)
Dm7
Ooh, some - one,
I fi - n'lly found some - one.
B♭maj9
F/G
Ooh,
Verse:
C(9)
Am7
I did - n't mind.
Ba - by, that's fine,
Did I keep you wait - ing?
I a - pol - o - gize.
Fmaj9
Fm6
just to know you were mine.
I will wait for - ev - er just to know you were mine.
You know,

C(9)
Am7
Are you sure it looks right?
Is - n't it too tight?
I love your hair,
I love what you wear.
Fmaj9
Fm6
I can't wait for the rest of my life!
Well, you're ex - cep - tion - al!
Chorus:
G♭(9)
This is it! Oh, I fi - n'lly
C♭maj9
C♭m6
G♭(9)
found some - one, some - one to share my life. I fi - n'lly

C♭maj9
C♭m6
G♭(9)
found the one_ to be with ev - 'ry_ night._ 'Cause what -
B♭7sus
B♭7
E♭m
ev - er I do,_ it's just got to be you.
D
G♭/D♭
Oh_ yeah, my life has just_ be - gun,_ I fi - n'lly
A♭m7/D♭
E♭7sus
E♭7
found some - one._ And what -

A♭m7
G♭/B♭
ev - er I do, it's just got to be you. Ooh, my
A♭m7/D♭
life has just be - gun, I fi - n'lly
G♭(9)
C♭maj9
found some - one.
G♭(9)

THIS KISS

Words and Music by
ROBIN LERNER, ANNIE ROBOFF
and BETH NIELSEN CHAPMAN

Moderately, with double-time feel ♩ = 64
B G♯m7 A F♯m7
mf
B G♯m7 A F♯m7
Verse:
B G♯m7 A F♯m7
1. I don't want an-oth-er heart-break. I don't need an-oth-er turn to cry, no.
2. Cin-der-el-la said to Snow White, "How does love get so off course?" Oh.
B G♯m7 A F♯m7
I don't want to learn the hard way. Ba-by, hel-lo, oh no, good-bye.
All I want-ed was a white knight with a good heart, soft touch, fast horse.

B
G♯m7
A
F♯m7
But you got me like a rock - et shoot-ing straight a - cross the sky.
Ride me off in - to the sun - set, ba - by, I'm for - ev - er yours.
Chorus:
E
E/G♯
A
B
It's the way you love me. It's a feel - ing like this.
It's cen - trif - u - gal mo - tion. It's per - pet - u - al bliss.
It's that piv - ot - al mo - ment. It's, ah, im - pos - si - ble. un - think - a - ble.
C♯m7
This kiss, this kiss, un - stop - a - ble. un - sink - a - ble.

E
E/G♯
1.
A
C♯m7
B
2.
A
C♯m7
B
This kiss, this kiss.
Bridge:
C
Am7
D/F♯
G
You can kiss me in the moon-light, on the roof-top, un-der the sky, oh.
C
Am7
D/F♯
G
You can kiss me with the win-dows o-pen while the rain comes blow-in' in-side, oh.
C
C/B
Am7
G
D/F♯
G
Kiss me in sweet, slow mo-tion. Let's let ev-'ry-thing slide.
F♯m7
F♯m7/B
You got me float-ing, you got me fly-ing.

F♯
F♯/A♯
B
C♯
It's the way you love me.
It's a feel-ing like this.
It's cen-trif-u-gal mo-tion.
It's per-pet-u-al bliss.
It's that piv-ot-al mo-ment.
D♯m7
It's, ah, sub-lim-i-nal.
This kiss, this kiss.
It's crim-i-nal.
This kiss, this kiss.
It's the way you love me,
Repeat and fade
ba - by.
It's the way you love me, dar - ling.

I LOVE THE WAY YOU LOVE ME

Words and Music by
VICTORIA SHAW and
CHUCK CANNON

Slowly ♩ = 84
Guitar (Capo 1st Fret):
Keyboard:
G
A♭
Am
B♭m
mf
(with pedal)

Bm/D
Cm/E♭
Am/D
B♭m/E♭
Verse:
G
A♭
1. I like the feel_ of your name on my lips;___ and
I like the way_ your eyes dance when you laugh;___ and

Em
Fm
C(2)
D♭(2)
I like the sound_ of your sweet,___ gen - tle_ kiss;_ the way that your fin - gers_ run__
how you en - joy_ your two hour___ bath;_ and how you con - vinced_ me to dance_

1.
C/D
D♭/E♭
D
E♭
C/D
D♭/E♭
D
E♭
through my hair; and how your scent lin - gers e - ven when you're not there. 2. And
in the rain with
2.3.
C/D
D♭/E♭
D
E♭
C/D
D♭/E♭
D
E♭
Chorus:
C(2)
D♭(2)
ev - 'ry - one watch - ing like we were in - sane. But I love
cresc.
f
C/D
D♭/E♭
D
E♭
G
A♭
the way you love me,
C(2)
D♭(2)
D
E♭
G
A♭
strong and wild, slow and eas - y, heart and soul,

C
G/B
Am7
C/D
(D)
D♭
A♭/C
B♭m7(4)
D♭/E♭
(E♭)
so com - plete - ly. I love the way you love
To Coda
1.
D.S.
G
Am
Bm/D
Am/D
A♭
B♭m
Cm/E♭
B♭m/E♭
me.
2.
Bridge:
C(2)
D
D♭(2)
E♭
And I could list a mil - lion things
G
C
A♭
D♭
I love to like a - bout you, but they all come down to

Verse 3:
I like to imitate ol' Jerry Lee
While you roll your eyes when I'm slightly off key.
And I like the innocent way that you cry
At sappy, old movies you've seen hundreds of times.
(To Chorus:)

I SWEAR

By
GARY BAKER and FRANK MYERS
Moderately slow
D♭
4fr.
B♭m7
Fm7
mf
Pedal throughout
E♭m7/A♭
4fr.
A♭
4fr.
D♭
4fr.
B♭m7
Fm7
E♭m7/A♭
4fr.
A♭
4fr.
D♭
4fr.
G♭/B♭
A♭/C
I see the ques - tions in your eyes,
(See additional lyrics)
D♭
4fr.
G♭
A♭
4fr.
B♭m
I know what's weigh - ing on your mind, but you can be sure

G♭
E♭m7/A♭
A♭
D♭
4fr.
I know my part. I'll stand be - side
G♭/B♭
A♭/C
D♭
G♭
A♭
you through the years, you'll on - ly cry those hap - py tears.
B♭m
D♭/A♭
E♭/G
And though I'll make mis - takes, I'll nev - er break your heart.
E♭m7/A♭
A♭
D♭
B♭m7
I swear, by the moon and the stars in the sky,

Fm7
G♭
A♭
4fr.
D♭
4fr.
I'll be there. I swear, like a sha-
B♭m7
Fm7
G♭
A♭
4fr.
dow that's by your side, I'll be there. For
E♭m7
6fr.
E♭m7/A♭
4fr.
A♭
4fr.
E♭m7
6fr.
To Coda
bet-ter or worse, till death do us part, I'll love you with ev - er - y beat
1.
E♭m7/A♭
4fr.
A♭
4fr.
D♭
4fr.
B♭m7
of my heart, I swear.

Additional lyrics

2. I'll give you everything I can,
I'll build your dreams with these two hands,
And we'll hang some memories on the wall.
And when there's silver in your hair,
You won't have to ask if I still care,
'Cause as time turns the page my love won't age at all.
(To Chorus)

I WANT YOU TO NEED ME

Words and Music by
DIANE WARREN
Slowly ♩ = 76
E♭(9)
p
𝄋 Verse:
D♭
G♭
A♭
1.3. I wan - na be the face you see__ when you close your eyes.
2. I wan - na be the eyes that look__ deep in - to your soul.
mf
D♭
G♭
A♭
I wan-na be the touch you need_ ev - 'ry sin - gle night.______
I wan-na be the world to you._ I just want it all.______

B♭
E♭/G
E♭
A♭
E♭/G
I wan-na be your fan - ta - sy, and be your re - al - i - ty, and ev -
I wan-na be your deep - est kiss, the an-swer to your ev - 'ry wish, and all
F5
B♭/D
Chorus:
E♭
'ry - thing be - tween.
you ev - er need.
I want you to need me like the
F/B♭
B♭
Cm7
air you breathe. I want you to feel me in
F/B♭
B♭
E♭
ev - 'ry - thing. I want you to see me in your

To Coda
1.
B♭/D
Cm7
B♭
A♭
F5
ev - 'ry dream, I want you to taste me, feel me, breathe me, need me. I want you to need
E♭
2.
F5
E♭
me, need me like I need you.
need me. I want you to need me, need me. 'Coz
Bridge:
Cm7
B♭/D
I need you more than you could know. And
E♭
F
I need you to nev-er, nev - er let me go. And

Cm7
B♭
I need to be deep in - side your heart. I
D.S.𝄋 al Coda
A♭
Fsus
F
just wan - na be ev - 'ry-where you are.
Coda F5
need me. I want you to need
E♭
F/B♭
B♭
me like the air you breathe. I want you to feel

Cm7
F/B♭
B♭
me in ev - 'ry - thing. I want you to see
Cm7
B♭/D
Cm7
B♭
A♭
me in your ev - 'ry dream, I want you to taste me, feel me, breathe me,
F5
E♭(9)
need me. I want you to need me, need me like I need you,
like I need you, like I need you.
rit.

I WILL ALWAYS LOVE YOU

A
F♯m7
D
E
I will al - ways love you. I
will al - ways love you.
1. A
D(addE)
A/C♯
Bm7
A/B
Bm7
2. A
D/A
A
E6
Bm/E
D.S. al Coda
Bit - ter you. I
Coda
Dmaj7
E
B
G♯m7
4fr.
F♯
love. And I will al - ways love
f
a tempo

B G♯m7 4fr. C♯m7 4fr. F♯ B G♯m7 4fr. E F♯
you. I will al - ways love you. I will al - ways love
B G♯m7 4fr. C♯m7 4fr. F♯ B G♯m7 4fr. E F♯
you. I will al - ways love you. I will al-ways love
B G♯m7 4fr. E F♯ E(addF♯)
No Chord
you. I, I will al - ways love you.
mp
B/D♯ C♯m7/F♯ 9fr. F♯7 B(addC♯) 4fr.
I'll al-ways, I'll al - ways love you.
rit.

I WILL COME TO YOU

Words and Music by
ISAAC HANSON, TAYLOR HANSON,
ZACHARY HANSON, BARRY MANN
and CYNTHIA WEIL

Verse:
G♭
G♭/A♭
D♭
B♭m
come to you, oh, come to you.
1. Oh, some - times, when all your dreams may have
2. Oh, na, na, na, na, na, na, na, na,
D♭
A♭/C
seen bet - ter days,
na, na, na, na.
and when you don't know how or why, but you
Na, na, na, na, na, na, na, na,
E♭m7/A♭
G♭maj7
lost your way.
na, na, na.
Have no fear when your tears are fall - in',
'Cause e - ven if we can't be to - geth - er,
Fm7
E♭m7
I will hear your spir - it call - in'.
we'll be friends now and for - ev - er.
And I swear that I'll be there come

1.
2.
G♭/A♭
A♭
what may.
When you
what may.
When the
D♭
E♭m
B♭m
night is dark and storm-y, you won't have to reach out for me, oh, I will
G♭
E♭m7/A♭
come to you, oh, I will come to you, oh.
Bridge:
E♭m7
We all need some-bod-y we can turn to, oh,

A♭/C
D♭
some - one who'll al - ways under - stand.
E♭m7
B♭m
So if you feel that your soul is dy - ing, and you need the strength to keep try - ing,
G♭
A♭sus
A♭
I'll reach out and take your hand, oh.
Cm
A♭
E♭/B♭
B♭
E♭
Na, na, na, na, na, na, na, na, na, na, na, na. I'll reach out for your

Cm
A♭
B♭
E♭
hand.
Na, na, na, na, na, na, na, na, na, na, na, na.
Solo
I'll come to
E♭/B♭
B♭
E♭
B♭
you, oh. When you have no light to guide you, and no
Fm
Cm
A♭
A♭/B♭
B♭
one to walk be - side you, I will come to you, oh, I will come

Eb
Bb
Eb
Bb
to you.
When the night is dark and storm - y, you won't
Fm
Cm
Ab
Ab/Bb
Bb
have to reach out for me, oh, I will come to you, oh, come
Eb
Ab
Fm7/Bb
Eb
Bb
to you. I will come to you, oh, I will come to you, oh, oh,
molto rit. e dim.
mp
a tempo
Fm
Cm
Ab6
Fm7/Bb
Eb
oh, oh, oh. Ooh, I come to you, ah, I will come to you.
molto rit. e dim.
p

I'LL STILL LOVE YOU MORE

Words and Music by
DIANE WARREN

F♯m7
D
C♯m7
F♯m7
D
You could say you could-n't live one day with-out me.
You could say all of your thoughts
C♯m7
G13
F♯m7
D
C♯m7
are thoughts a-bout me.
You could think no oth-er love could be as strong,
Bm7
Bm7/E
but you'd be wrong,
you'd be wrong.
If you
Chorus:
A
F♯m7
D
say that you love me more than an-y-bod-y, than an-y-one's ev-er been loved
D♯m7(♭5)
D
Bm7
be-fore, as much as you love me, ba-by, I'll still love you, ba-by,

1.
Bm7/E
E/F♯
F♯m7
Bm7/E
A
I'll still love you more.
F♯m7
D
2. A
And for
Bridge:
Dmaj7
A/C♯
Dmaj7
ev - 'ry kiss, I'll kiss you back a hun-dred times. And for ev - 'ry-thing you do, I'll just do
A/C♯
Bm7
C♯m7
F♯m7
more. And for all the love you give, I'll give you so much back, you'll see. Got
D
Bm7/E
C♯m7/F♯
so much love for you in - side me. If you

Verse 2:
Ask me just what I'd do for you;
I'll tell you that I would do anything.
Ask if this heart beats true for you;
I'll show you a truer heart could never be.
You could say there's not a star that you won't bring me.
You could say there'll be no day that you won't need me.
You could think no other love could last as long,
But you'd be wrong,
You'd be wrong.
(To Chorus:)

I'M YOUR ANGEL

Words and Music by
R. KELLY

I'm Your Angel - 6 - 1

C(9) G C/E

No riv - er's too wide ___ for you to make it a - cross. All ___ you have ___
You have ev - 'ry - thing ___ and you're still lone - ly. It ___ don't have ___

F Gsus G E/G♯

___ to do ___ is ___ be - lieve ___ it when ___ you pray. And
___ to be ___ this way. Let me show you ___ a bet - ter day. And

Am E7/G♯ C/G D9/F♯

then you will see, ___ the morn-ing will come, ___ and ev - er - y day ___ will be bright as the sun. ___
then you will see, ___ the morn-ing will come, ___ and all of your days ___ will be bright as the sun. ___ So

Dm7 C(9)/E F/A G/B

All of your fears, ___ cast them on me. ___ I just want you to see.
all of your fears, ___ just cast them on me. ___ How can I make you see? } I'll be your ___

Chorus:
C
Am7
Gsus
G
C/E
cloud up in the sky. I'll be your shoul - der when you cry. I'll hear your
F
F/A
Gsus
G
F/A
G/B
3
voic - es when you call me. I am your an - gel. And when all
C
Am7
Gsus
G
C/E
hope is gone, I'm here. No mat - ter how far you are, I'm near. It makes no
F
F/A
Gsus
G
3
dif - fer - ence who you are, I am your an - gel. I'm your

1.
F
C
an - gel.
2.
Bridge:
F
C
an - gel.
And when it's time to face the storm,
Cmaj7
Em7
Dm7
C
Cmaj7
I'll be right by your side.
Grace will keep us safe and warm,
F
Em7
Dm7
Am7
E7/G♯
and I know we will sur - vive.
And when it seems as if your end

C/G
D9/F♯
F
is drawing near, don't you dare give up the fight. Just put your
(The end is drawing near.)
G
E♭m7/A♭
N.C.
trust beyond the sky. I'll be your
Chorus:
D
Bm7
Asus
A
D/F♯
cloud up in the sky. I'll be your shoulder when you cry. I'll hear your

G
G/B
Asus
A
G/B
A/C♯
voic - es when you call me. I am your an - gel. And when all
D
Bm7
Asus
A
D/F♯
hope is gone, I'm here. No mat - ter how far you are, I'm near. It makes no
G
G/B
Asus
A
Repeat ad lib. and fade
dif - fer - ence who you are, I am your an - gel. I'll be your

I'VE DREAMED OF YOU

Words and Music by
ANN HAMPTON CALLAWAY
and ROLF LOVLAND

Slowly, freely ♩ = 72
C5
mp
(with pedal)
C
Fmaj7
1. I've
Verse:
Cmaj7
Fmaj7
Cmaj7
dreamed of you, al - ways feel - ing you were there.
just when I thought love had passed me by, we met.
simile

Fmaj7
Cmaj7
Fmaj7
And all my life I have searched for you ev - 'ry -
That first look in your eyes, I can't for -
Am7
F
where. I caught your smile in the
get. You melt - ed me with your
Em
F
B♭
morn-ing sun, I heard your whis-per on the breeze at night. I
ten-der touch. I felt all fear and sor-row slip a - way. Now,
C/G
Fmaj7
1.
Cmaj7
prayed one day that your arms would hold me tight.
here we stand, hand in hand, this bless-ed

2.
Fmaj7
C
G/B
F/A
Fm/A♭
2. And
day.
C/G
Am
Dm
Fmaj7/G
G7
Verse:
C
Cmaj7
3. I
prom - ise you,
as I
Fmaj7
C
Fmaj7
give to you
my heart,
that
Cmaj7
Fmaj7
Am7
noth - ing,
noth - ing in this
world
shall keep us
a - part.

F
Em
Come hap-pi-ly ev - er - af - ter, be___ the
F
B♭
C/G
man I'll love un-til the ver - y end. I've dreamed of you, my great
Fmaj7
Am7
C/G
love___ and my best friend.___ For
F
Em
F
God must know how I love you so; He's blessed us here to - day as man and

B♭
C/G
Fmaj7
C
wife. Come dream with me as I've dreamed of you all my life.
G/F
F
C/G
Fmaj7
Come dream with me as I have dreamed of you all my
N.C.
C5
C
life.

IF TOMORROW NEVER COMES

Words and Music by
KENT BLAZY and GARTH BROOKS

D
Am7
D
C
would she ev - er doubt the way I feel a - bout her in my
G
3
C/G
G
Chorus:
C
heart.
If to - mor - row nev-er
comes,
will she know how much I
G
D
Am7
loved her?
Did I try in ev - ery
way
to show her ev - ery - day
D
C
G
Am7
G/B
that she's my on-ly one?
And if my time on earth were
C
D
Em7
Bm7
through,
and she must face this world with - out me,

Verse 2:
'Cause I've lost loved ones in my life.
Who never knew how much I loved them.
Now I live with the regret
That my true feelings for them never were revealed.
So I made a promise to myself
To say each day how much she means to me
And avoid that circumstance
Where there's no second chance to tell her how I feel. ('Cause)
(To Chorus:)

IF YOU EVER HAVE FOREVER IN MIND

Words and Music by
VINCE GILL and TROY SEALS

B♭
Bdim7
F
Dm7
I may be a fool to love by the
Gm7
C7
F
B♭7
F
C7
rules. I want it to last. If you
Chorus:
F
Fmaj7
Cm7
F7
B♭
ev-er (if you ev-er) have for-ev - er in mind,
C7
I'll be here and eas - y to
F
C7
F
Fmaj7
find. If your heart (if your heart) is-n't

Verse 2:
Music has ended, still you wanna dance.
I know that feeling, I can't take the chance.
You live for the moment; no future, no past.
I may be a fool to live by the rules.
I want it to last.
(To Chorus:)

IN THIS LIFE

Words and Music by
MIKE REID and ALLEN SHAMBLIN

G7sus
C
3
With one hon - est touch you set me free.
Let the
cresc.
Chorus:
Dm
G/B
C
F
world stop turn - ing, let the sun stop burn - ing. Let them
mf
Dm
G7sus
G
C/E
tell me love's not worth go - ing through.
If it
F
G/B
C
C/E
F
all falls a - part, I will know deep in my heart the

Verse 2:
For every mountain I have climbed.
Every raging river crossed,
You were the treasure that I longed to find.
Without your love I would be lost.
(To Chorus:)

JUST TO HEAR YOU SAY THAT YOU LOVE ME

Words and Music by
DIANE WARREN

C
D
D
E
C
D
noth-ing in this world I won't try,
no
lim - it to what I'd do to
B7sus
C♯7sus
Chorus:
E
F♯
F♯m/E
G♯m/F♯
make you mine.
1.2. I'd climb right
(3.) you. (Instrumental solo...
up to the sky,
A
B
E/G♯
F♯/A♯
F♯m7
G♯m7
E
F♯
take down the stars just to
be in your arms, ba - by.
I'd go and
F♯m/E
G♯m/F♯
A
B
B7
C♯7
cap-ture the moon, that's what
I would do
just to hear you say that you love

1.
E
To Coda
B7
E
Am7/D
F♯
C♯7
F♯
Bm7/E
me.
Just to hear you say that you love me.
2.
Bridge:
B7
C♯m7
B
C♯7
D♯m7
C♯
Just to hear you say that you love me for the rest of my life.
Ba-by,
C♯m7
G♯m7
E♭m7
D♯m7
A♯m7
Fm7
love me for the rest of all time.
Just say the word and I'll
F♯m7/B
D.S. 𝄋 al Coda
G♯m7/C♯
give you my world.
There's noth-ing I won't do,
ba - by, just to be with

Coda
B
C♯
...end solo)
Chorus:
F♯
A♭
I'd climb right
G♯m/F♯
B♭m/A♭
up to the sky,
B
D♭
take down the stars
F♯/A♯
A♭/C
just to
G♯m7
B♭m7
be in your arms, ba - by.
F♯
A♭
I'd go and
G♯m/F♯
B♭m/A♭
cap-ture the moon, that's what
B
C♯
I would do
C♯7
E♭7
just to hear you say that you love

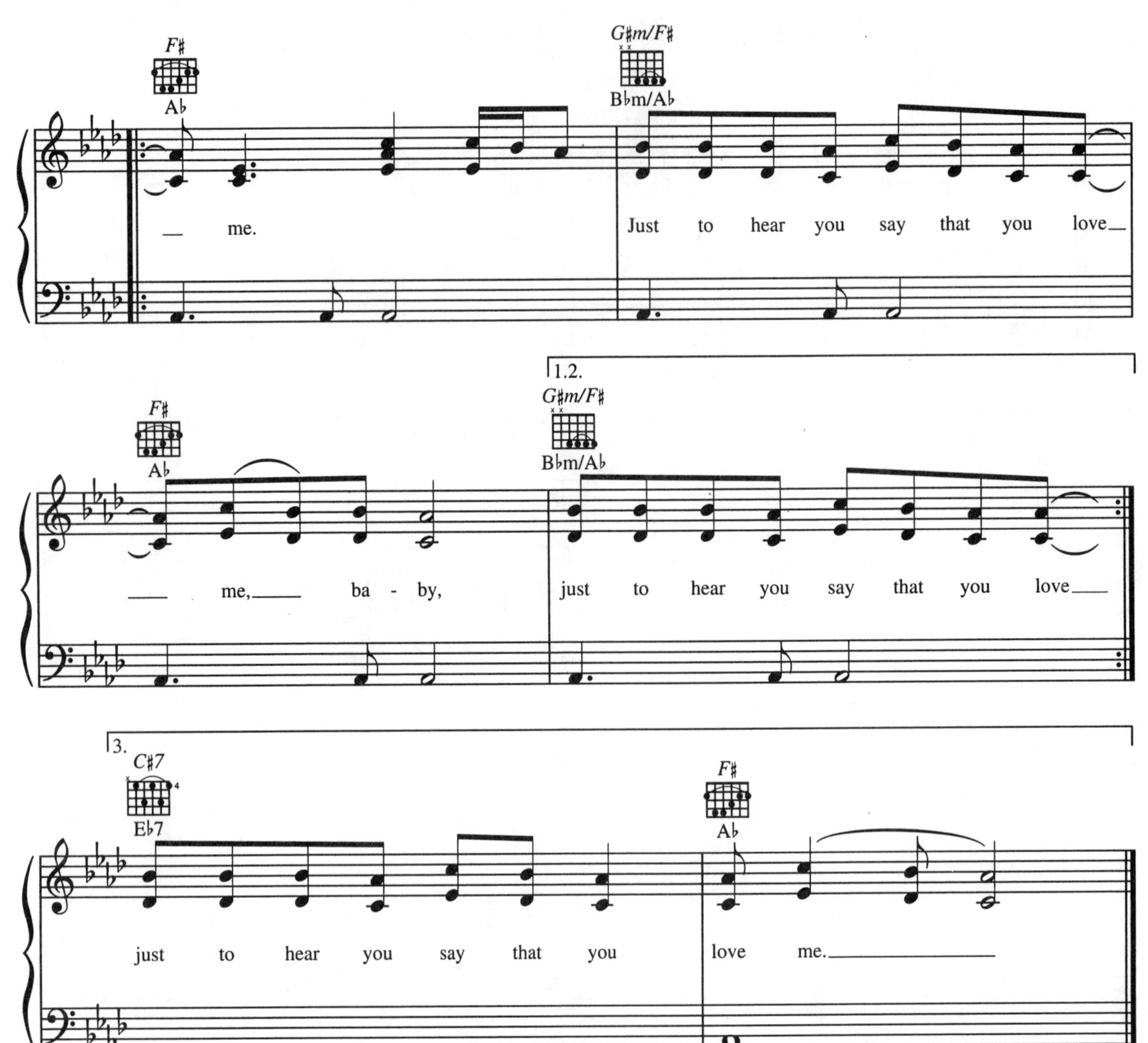

Verse 2:
If I could taste your kiss,
There'd be no sweeter gift heaven could offer, baby.
I want to be the one
Living to give you love.
I'd walk across this world just to be
Close to you, 'cos I want you close to me.
(To Chorus:)

LOVE CAN MOVE MOUNTAINS

Words and Music by
DIANE WARREN

A♭
B♭sus
B♭
B♭sus
B♭
to do we can do now. There ain't noth - ing in our way, ba - by.
the sky, just be - lieve it, be - lieve in you and I, ba - by.
B♭/C
A/C♯
Dm7
Noth-ing our love could-n't rise a - bove. We can get through the night, we can
If we got love that is strong e - nough we can do an - y - thing, make it
Gm7
get to the light. Long as we got our love to light the way.
through an - y - thing. 'Cause through it all love will al - ways find a way.
B♭/C
With a lit - tle faith,

Chorus:

F Ab2 Bbsus Bb

just a lit - tle trust, if you be - lieve in love, love

Ab Bb F Ab2

can move moun - tains. Be - lieve in your heart and feel, feel it in your soul and love,

Bbsus Bb Ab Bb 1. F Gm7/F

love can, love can move moun - tains.

Fm7 Bb/F

2.
F
Fm7
B♭sus
B♭
moun - tains.
(Trust)
You've got to feel it, ba - by.
(Love)
(Love
A♭
B♭
F
Fm7
can, love can move
moun - tains.)
You've got to feel it, ba - by.
(Trust)
B♭sus
B♭
A♭
B♭
F
Fm7
(Love)
(Love can, love can move
moun - tains.)
B♭sus
B♭
A♭
B♭
(Trust)
You've got to feel it, ba - by.
(Love)
(Love can, love can move it.)

F
Gm7/F
Fm7
You be - lieve in me, I'll be - lieve in
B♭/F
Gm7/C
you. If we be - lieve in each oth - er, noth - ing we can't do.
Am7/D
If we got love that is strong e - nough love will find a
Gm7/C
D.S. 𝄋 and fade (no repeats)
way. With a lit - tle faith.

THE KEEPER OF THE STARS

Words and Music by
DICKEY LEE, DANNY MAYO
and KAREN STALEY

D
A/C♯
Bm
Now, I just can't be - lieve you're in my life.
I know I don't de - serve a trea - sure like you.
G
D/F♯
Heav-en's smil-in' down on me
There real - ly are no words
Em
A7sus
A
N.C.
D/F♯
as I look at you to - night.
to show my grat - i - tude.
I tip my
mf
Chorus:
G
A
F♯m
hat to the keep - er of the stars.

G
Em
A7
He sure knew what he was do - in'
when he joined these two
D
D/F♯
G
hearts.
I hold ev - 'ry - thing
A
F♯m
G
D/F♯
Em
when I hold you in my arms.
I've got all I'll ev-er need
1.
A
G
D
A7sus
thanks to the keep-er of the stars.
dim.
mp

2.
A
D
thanks to the keep - er of___ the stars.__
dim.
A/C♯
Bm
mp
It was_ no ac - ci - dent,_ me find - ing
G
D/F♯
you. Some-one had a hand_ in it___
Em
A7sus
D
A7sus
D
long be - fore_ we_ ev - er knew.
a tempo
dim. e rit.
p

KISSING YOU
(Love Theme From "ROMEO + JULIET")

Words and Music by
DES'REE and TIM ATACK

Kissing You - 4 - 1

Dm7 C(9) Am7 Em7 Am7 C/G Dm7 Am7 G/B
Heav - ing heart is full of pain, oh, oh, the
Chorus:
C G/B G♯dim7 Am7 Dm7 Am7 G/B
ach - ing. 'Cause I'm kiss - ing
C G/B Am7 C/G Dm7 Am7 G/B C G/B Am7 C/G
you, oh. I'm kiss-ing you.
Verse:
Dm7 C(9) Am7 Em7 Am7 C/G Dm7 Am7 G/B
2. Touch me deep, pure, and true, gift to me for-

Chorus:
C G/B Am7 C/G Dm7 Am7 G/B C G/B Am7 C/G
ev - er. 'Cause I'm kiss - ing you, oh.
Dm7 Am7 G/B C G/B Am7 C/G Dm7 C
I'm kiss - ing you.
Am7 C/G Dm7 C
Am7 C/G Fmaj7 G Am7 G/B

Dm9
C
G/B
Am7
Dm7
Am7
freely
rit.
Where are you now?
C
G/B
Am7
C/G
Dm7
Am7
C
G/B
Am7
C/G
Where are you now? 'Cause
Dm7
Am7
C
G/B
Am7
C/G
Dm7
Am7
G/B
I'm kiss-ing you. I'm kiss-ing
C(9)
G/B
Am9
you, oh.

LOST IN YOU

Words and Music by
TOMMY SIMS, GORDON KENNEDY
and WAYNE KIRKPATRICK

Lost in You - 4 - 1

F
Am7
D7sus
Dm7
You are my god - send that
That I should dare to
C/B♭
B♭
F/G
Gm7
C6
C7
I've been for - ev - er dream - ing of, my
swear to sur - ren - der ev - er - more. That's
F/G
Gm7
B♭m/D♭
an - gel from a - bove.
what I came here for.
Heav - en knows
Chorus:
Gm7
Fmaj7
C/D
Dm7
Gm7
I'm head o - ver heels and it shows. I've played

Fmaj7 C/D Dm7 Gm7 Am7 B♭maj7 A7
(harmony tacet 1x)
(tutti)
ev - 'ry field, I sup - pose, but there's some - thing a - bout you. When
Dm C G/B Am7
To Coda 1.
B♭maj7
you're a - round, ba - by, I have found I get lost in
2.
N.C.
B♭maj7 C2
you. lost in a won - der - ful daze, lost
A♭/D♭ B♭/E♭ Gm9
in your won - der - ful ways. Heav - en knows.
(Inst. solo ad lib. . . .

Fmaj7 C/D Dm7 Gm9 F Dm7

Gm7 Am7 B♭maj7 A7 Dm C G/B

Oh, when you're a - round, ba - by, I

...end solo)

Am7 B♭maj7

D.S. 𝄋 al Coda

have found I get lost. Heav - en knows

Coda B♭maj7

lost in you.

rit.

LOVE IS ALL AROUND

Words and Music by
REG PRESLEY

♩= 85
F
B♭/F
F7
B♭/F
F
B♭/F
F7
B♭
Cm
E♭
F
1. I feel it in my fin - gers, I feel it in my toes. _
(Verse 2 see block lyric)
B♭
Cm
E♭
F
B♭
Cm
The love that's all a - round me

E♭ F B♭ Cm E♭ F
fr3 fr3 fr3
and so the feel - ing grows.__ It's
B♭ Cm E♭ F B♭ Cm
fr3 fr3 fr3
writ - ten on the wind, it's ev - 'ry - where I go,___
E♭ F B♭ E♭ E♭ F
fr3 fr3 fr3
so if you real - ly love me, come on and let it show._
B♭ Gm E♭ F
fr3 fr3

Eb
Cm
Eb
fr3
You know I love you, I al - ways will,
my mind's made up by the
Bb
Eb
Cm
way that I feel.
There's no be - gin - ning, there'll be no end,
'cause
F
1.
F7
on my love
you can de - pend.
Bb
Cm
Eb
Fsus4
F
Bb
Cm

2.
E♭
F
Fsus4
F7
B♭/F
F
B♭/F
2. I
Got to keep it mov - ing.
F7
B♭
Cm
It's writ - ten in the wind oh
E♭
Fsus4
F
B♭
Cm
ev - 'ry - where I go.
E♭
Fsus4
F
B♭
Cm
So if you real - ly love me,

Verse 2:
I see your face before me
As I lay on my bed;
I cannot get to thinking
Of all the things you said.
You gave your promise to me
And I gave mine to you;
I need someone beside me
In everything I do.

LOVE WILL KEEP US ALIVE

Words and Music by
JIM CAPALDI, PETER VALE
and PAUL CARRACK

D2(6)
You were search - ing for a place to hide.
The world is chang - ing right be - fore your eyes.
When we're hun - gry love will keep us a -
Esus
E
A2
live.
Lost and lone - ly,
Now I've found you,
(Instrumental solo . . .
F♯m11
now you've giv - en me the will to sur - vive.
there's no more emp - ti - ness in - side.
When we're
When we're

To Coda
1.
D2(6)
Esus
E
A2
hun - gry,
love will keep us a - live.
hun - gry,
love will keep us a - live.
2.3.
A2
2. Don't you
. . . end solo)
I would
Bridge:
D
F♯m7
die for you,
climb the high - est moun -

Bm7
- tain.
Ba - by,
there's noth-ing I
would-n't
1.
D.S. 𝄋
2.
D.S. 𝄋 al Coda
E
E/D
C♯m7
E/B
C♯m7
E/B
do.
3. Now, I've
4. I was
Coda
A2
F♯m11
When we're

D2(6)
Esus
E
A2
hun - gry,
love will keep us a - live.
F♯m11
D2(6)
Esus
When we're hun - gry,
love will keep us a - live.
A2
rit.

LOVE LIKE OURS

Lyrics by
ALAN and MARILYN BERGMAN

Music by
DAVE GRUSIN

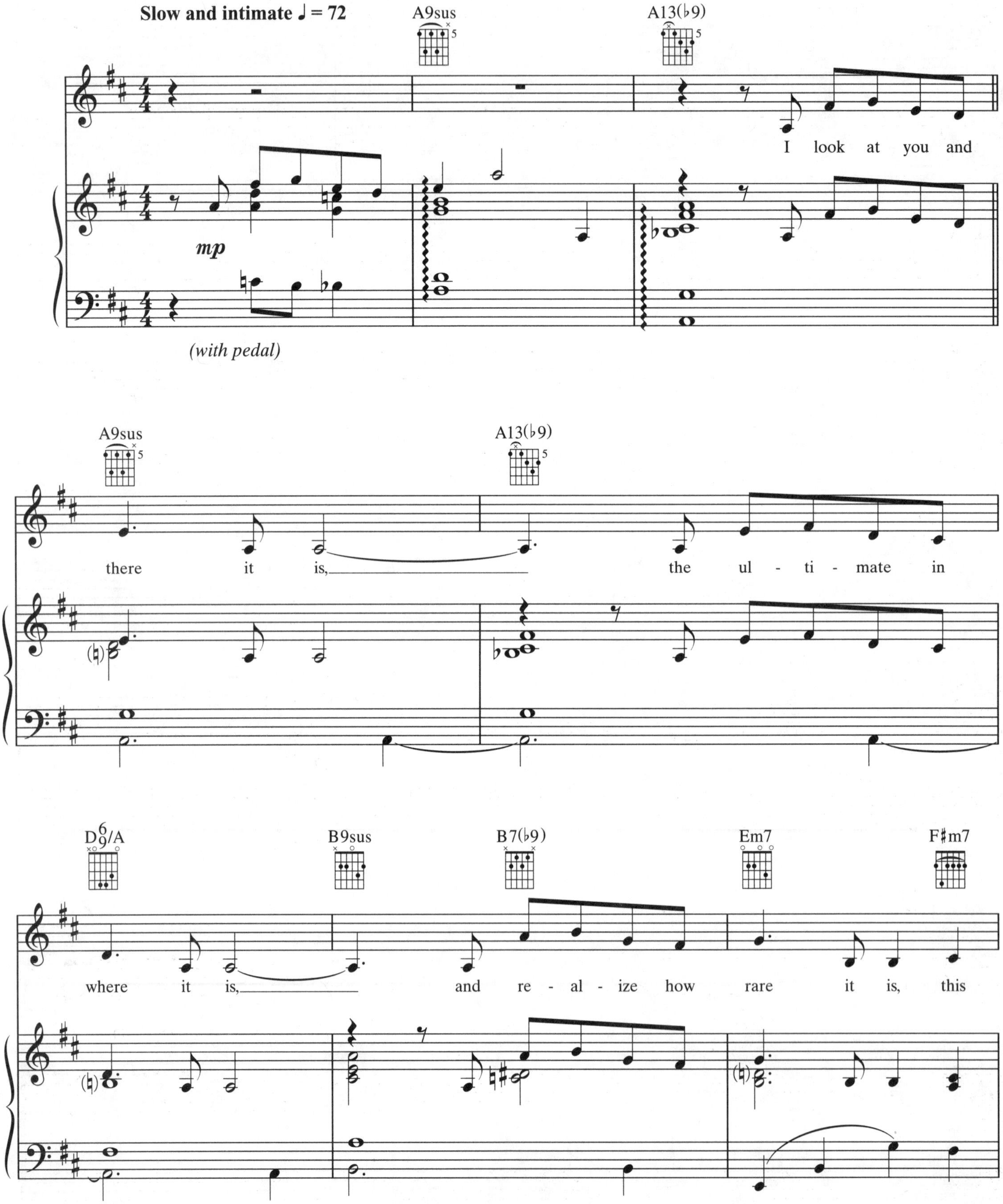

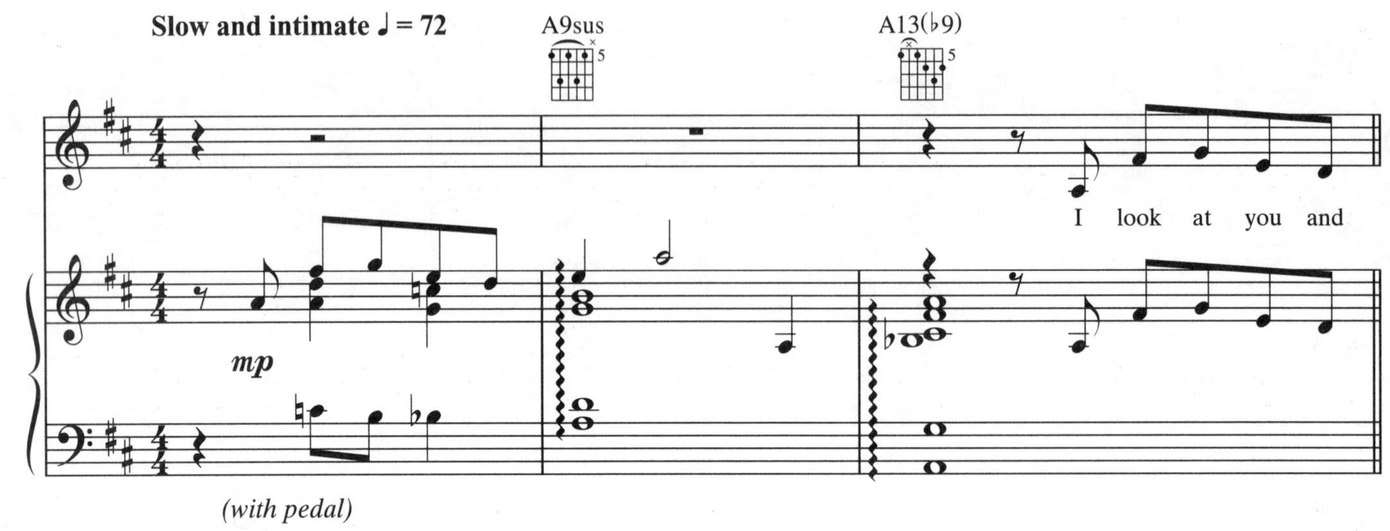

Slow and intimate ♩ = 72
A9sus
A13(♭9)
I look at you and
mp
(with pedal)
A9sus
A13(♭9)
there it is, the ul - ti - mate in
D6/9/A
B9sus
B7(♭9)
Em7
F♯m7
where it is, and re - al - ize how rare it is, this

Gm/A
A7(♭9)
D
A/C♯
F♯7
find - ing your love.
You try so man - y
Bm9
E9sus
C♯7/E♯
arms when you are lone - ly, to
F♯m9
B7sus(♭9)
B7(♭9)
C
find the one and on - ly.
One day you
C9/B♭
A11
Dmaj9/A
turn and she's he's there.
A - maz - ing how se -

A9sus
Am11
A7(♭9)
Dmaj9/A
rene it is, the shade of ev - er - green it is,
B11
B7(♭9)
Em7
F♯m7
ex - act - ly what we mean it is, and
A11
A7(♭9)
D11
D7/C
knew it would be.
Bm9
Bm9/A
G♯m9
When love like ours ar - rives,

C♯11(♭9)
C♯7(♭9)
D(9)/C
B9sus
B7(♭9)
we guard it with our lives.
What - ev - er goes a -
Em7
F♯m7
A11
A7(♭9)/G
F♯13sus
F♯7(♯5 ♭9)
stray, what rain - y day comes a - round,
B9sus
B7sus(♭9)
C9/B♭
a love like ours will keep us
A11
A13(♭9)
D(9)
safe and sound.
rit.

LOVING YOU IS ALL I KNOW

Words and Music by
DIANE WARREN

1.
2.3.
Dm7
Gsus
C
C
Lov - ing you is all I know. 2. I know. I don't
Chorus:
Fmaj7
C/E
know how the world keeps on spin - ning 'round. I don't know why the sky don't come fall - ing down. I just
E♭
B♭
C
know that I would die with - out your touch. I don't
Fmaj7
C/E
know why the tide needs to reach the shore. I just know I'll need you for for - ev - er - more.

1.
E♭
B♭
Gsus
G
D.S. 𝄋
And know - ing that, I guess I know e - nough. 3. I
2.
Verse 4:
Gsus
G
D
Dmaj7
Em11
nough. 4. I don't un - der - stand how the sun keeps shin - ing. And I don't
D
Dmaj7
Em11
Bm7
F♯7/A♯
un - der - stand why the sea - sons change. And I don't have a clue
D/A
E9/G♯
Em7
A7sus
A7
Bm
F♯7/A♯
what makes the riv - ers flow. Lov - ing you is all I know.

Verse 2:
I can't tell you why stars come out in the evening,
And I can't tell you where they go when they're gone.
And I don't have a clue what makes a flower grow.
Loving you is all I know.
(To Chorus:)

Verse 3:
I can't really say if there is a heaven,
But I feel like it's here when I feel you near me, baby.
I'm not sure of that much, but that's just how it goes.
Loving you is all I know.
(To Chorus:)

THE MAGIC OF LOVE

Lyrics by
ALAN and MARILYN BERGMAN

Music by
LIONEL RICHIE

The Magic of Love - 7 - 1

*Play chords 2nd time only.

Chorus:
E♭
A♭
E♭/G
But there's some - thing in - side us that
D♭
E♭
A♭
looks to the sun.
D♭
E♭
A♭
E♭/G
We dream that this light will guide us with
D♭
D♭/E♭
1.
E♭
love for ev - 'ry - one.

2.
Bridge:
E♭
C/E
Fm
E♭/G
Love is there for us, ev - 'ry -
In the sound of pray - ing. Lit - tle chil - dren
A♭
D♭
A♭
E♭
where for us. O - pen your heart.
pray - ing.
C/E
Fm
Love's in reach of us,
Con - stant as the moon glows,

E♭/G
A♭
D♭
here in each of us. Al -
or the way the grass grows.
Cm
B♭m7
Fm/A♭
E♭/G
ways and for - ev -
E♭
er.

Chorus 2:
B F♯/A♯ G♯m D♯m7/F♯ E B/D♯
Love is the riv - er that fills ev - 'ry
F♯ B F♯/A♯ G♯m D♯m7/F♯
sea, and the wa - ters that mir - ror the
E B/D♯ F♯sus F♯
way life should be.
Verse 3:
G♯m B/F♯ Emaj7 D♯ D♯7 G♯m
3. When the world is free of thun-der and the skies are

B/F♯
Emaj7
D♯7
G♯m
B/F♯
peace - ful a - bove,
once a - gain, we'll
Bright and beau - ti - ful.
Emaj7
D♯
D♯7
G♯m
B/F♯
know the won - der of the mag - ic pow - er of
Slowly
E
C♯m7
E/F♯
G♯m
love.
Oh, the mag - ic of love!

WHEN I NEED YOU

Words by
CAROLE BAYER SAGER

Music by
ALBERT HAMMOND

F/A
B♭m7
A♭
G♭/B♭
A♭/C
all that I so want to give you, it's on-ly a heart-beat a - way.___ When I
D♭
A♭/C
F/A
need love, I hold out my hands and I touch love, I nev-er knew there was so
B♭m7
A♭
much love, keep - ing me warm night and day.___
B♭m
A♭
Miles and miles of emp - ty space in be - tween us, a
It's not ea - sy when the road is your dri - ver,

B♭m
A♭
A♭/C
te - le - phone can't take the place of your smile, oh, but you
ho - ney that's a hea - vy load that we bear, oh, but you
D♭
B♭m7
E♭m7
D♭/E♭
E♭m7
D♭/E♭
know I won't be tra - vel - ling for ev - er, it's cold out, but hold out and
know I won't be tra - vel - ling a life - time, it's cold out, but hold out and
1.
E♭m7/A♭
D♭/A♭
E♭m7/A♭
A♭
G♭/B♭
A♭/C
D♭
do like I do. When I need you, I
G♭maj9
A♭/C
A♭
F7(♭9)
just close my eyes and I'm with you, and all that I so want to

B♭m7
A♭
give you ba-by, it's on-ly a heart-beat a - way.
2.
E♭m7/A♭ D♭/A♭ E♭m7/A♭ A♭ G♭/A♭ A♭7 D♭ D♭/C♭ G♭/B♭ G♭m/A♭
do like I do.
D♭/A♭ B♭m7 A♭ G♭ A♭ G♭/B♭ A♭/C
When I
D♭ A♭/C
need love, I hold out my hands and I touch love, and I

A♭
E♭m9
C♭maj7
B♭m7
F7
F7/A
B♭m7
never knew, oh never knew there was so much love,
A♭
E♭m9
A♭
keeping me warm night and day.
When I
D
Gmaj7
D
A/C♯
need you, I just close my eyes and I'm with you, and
Repeat ad lib. to fade
A
F♯7/A♯
Bm7
A
G/B
A/C♯
all that I so want to give you, it's only a heartbeat away.
When I

MORE THAN WORDS

Lyrics and Music by
BETTENCOURT, CHERONE

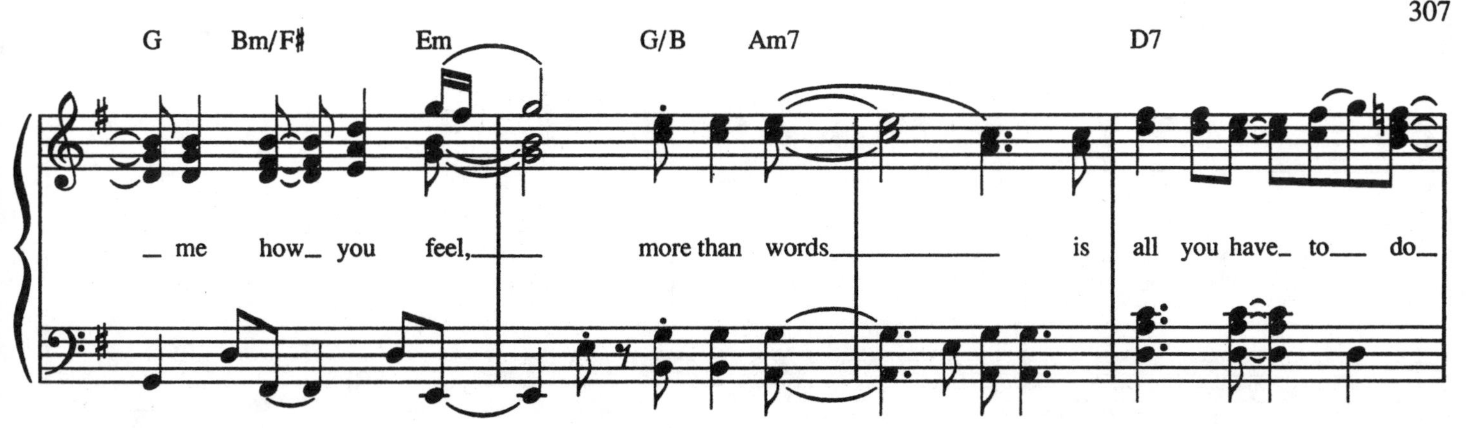
G Bm/F♯ Em G/B Am7 D7
_ me how_ you feel,_ more than words_ is all you have_ to_ do_

G7 G7/B C Cm G Em7
_ to make_ it_ real._ Then, you would - n't have_ to say_ that you love_

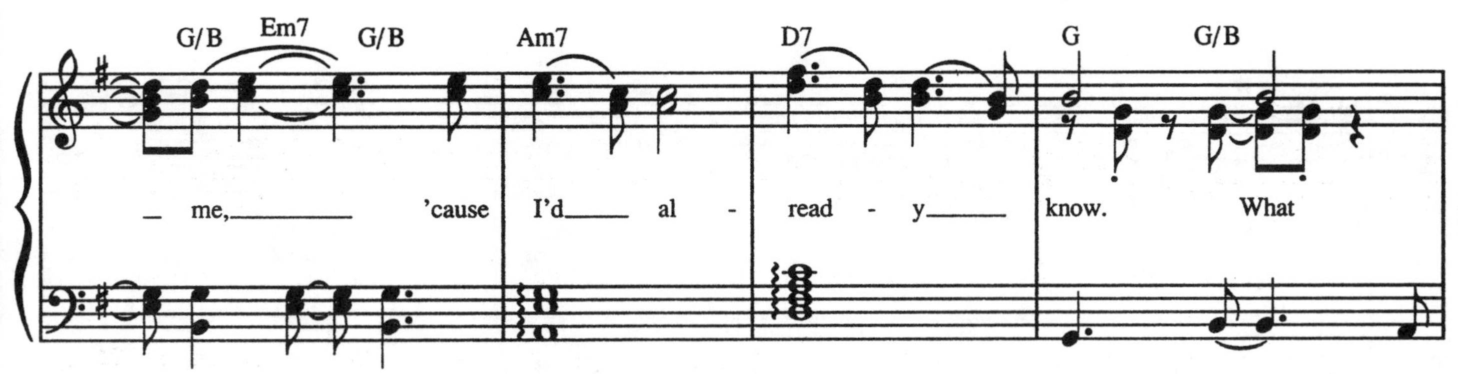
G/B Em7 G/B Am7 D7 G G/B
_ me,_ 'cause I'd_ al - read - y_ know. What

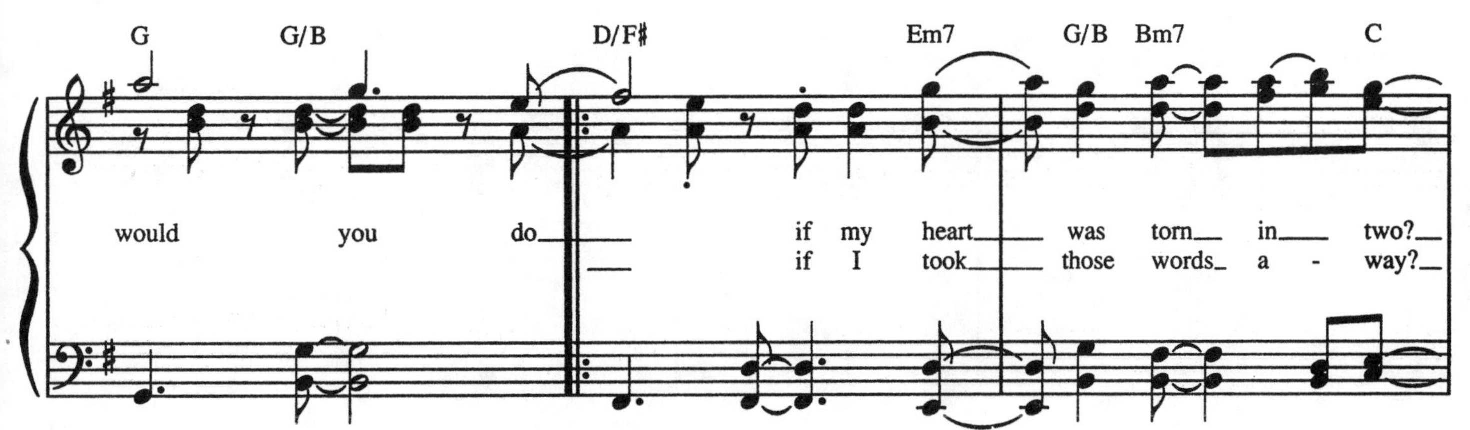
G G/B D/F♯ Em7 G/B Bm7 C
would you do_ if my heart_ was torn_ in_ two?_
_ if I took_ those words_ a - way?_

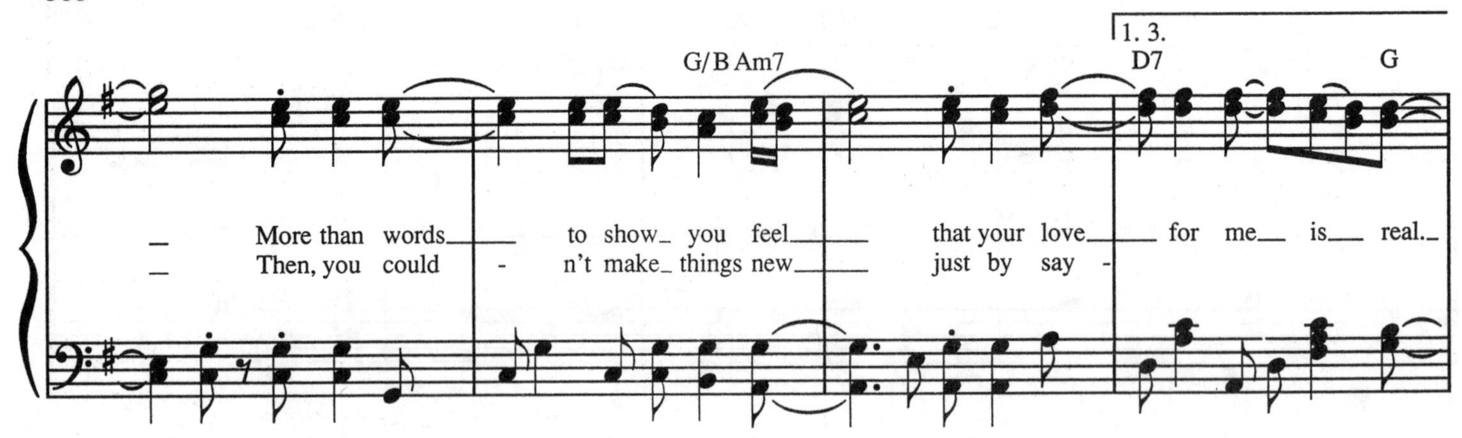
1. 3.
G/B Am7
D7
G
More than words to show you feel that your love for me is real.
Then, you could - n't make things new just by say -

G/B
G
G/B
2.
To Next Strain
D7
4.
D7
What would you say - in' "I love you."
- in' "I love you."

G
G/B
C(9)
G/B
Am7
G/B
C
(La di da da di da di dai dai da.

1.
D.S.
D
D7
G
G/B
C(9)
Am7
D7
) More than words.
La di da da di da.)

Verse 2:
Now that I have tried to talk to you
And make you understand.
All you have to do is close your eyes
And just reach out your hands.
And touch me, hold me close, don't ever let me go.
More than words is all I ever needed you to show.
Then you wouldn't have to say
That you love me 'cause I'd already know.
(To Chorus:)

From the Miramax Motion Picture "Music Of The Heart"

MUSIC OF MY HEART

Words and Music by
DIANE WARREN

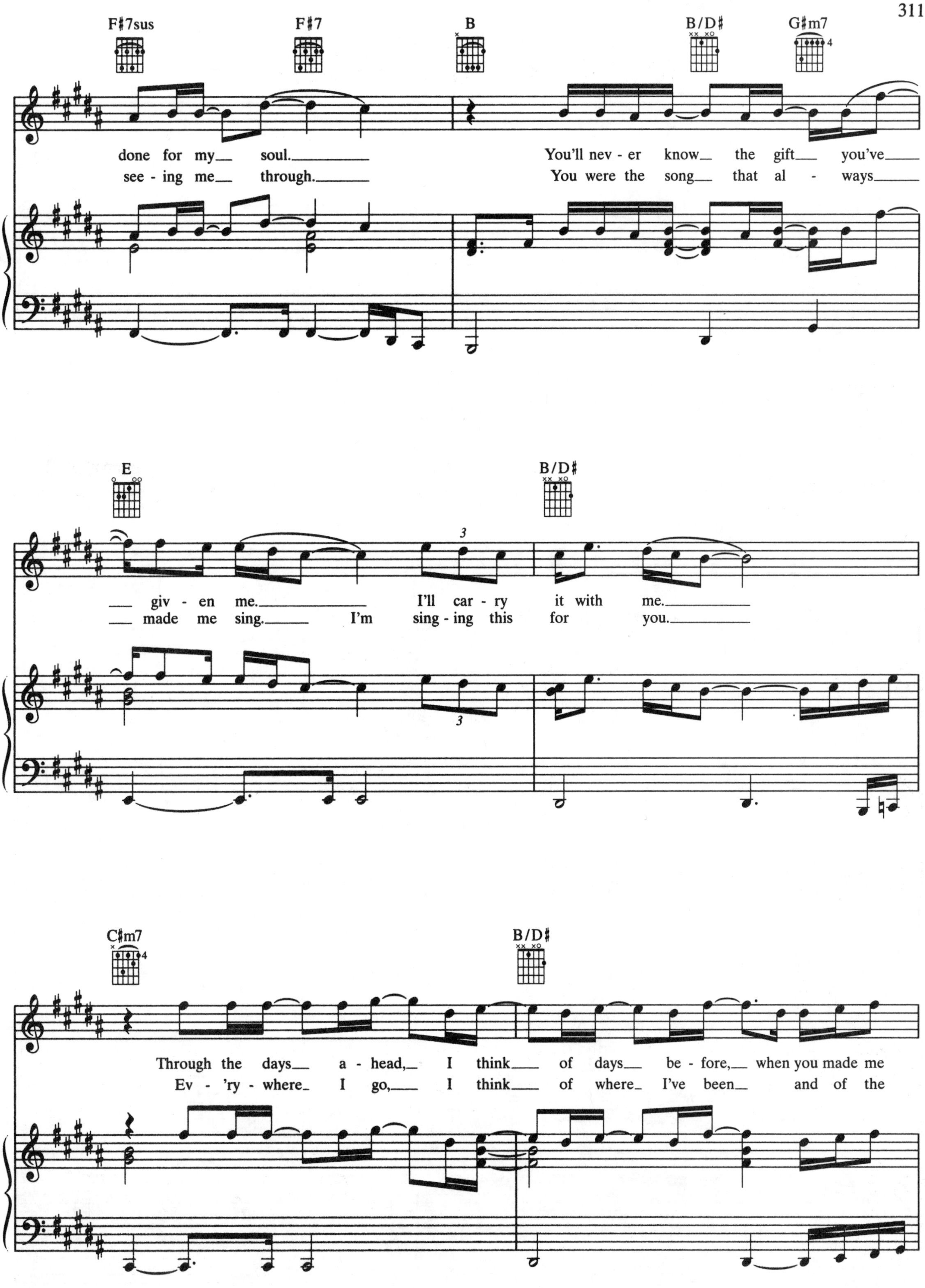

F♯7sus F♯7 B B/D♯ G♯m7

done for my soul. You'll nev - er know the gift you've
see - ing me through. You were the song that al - ways

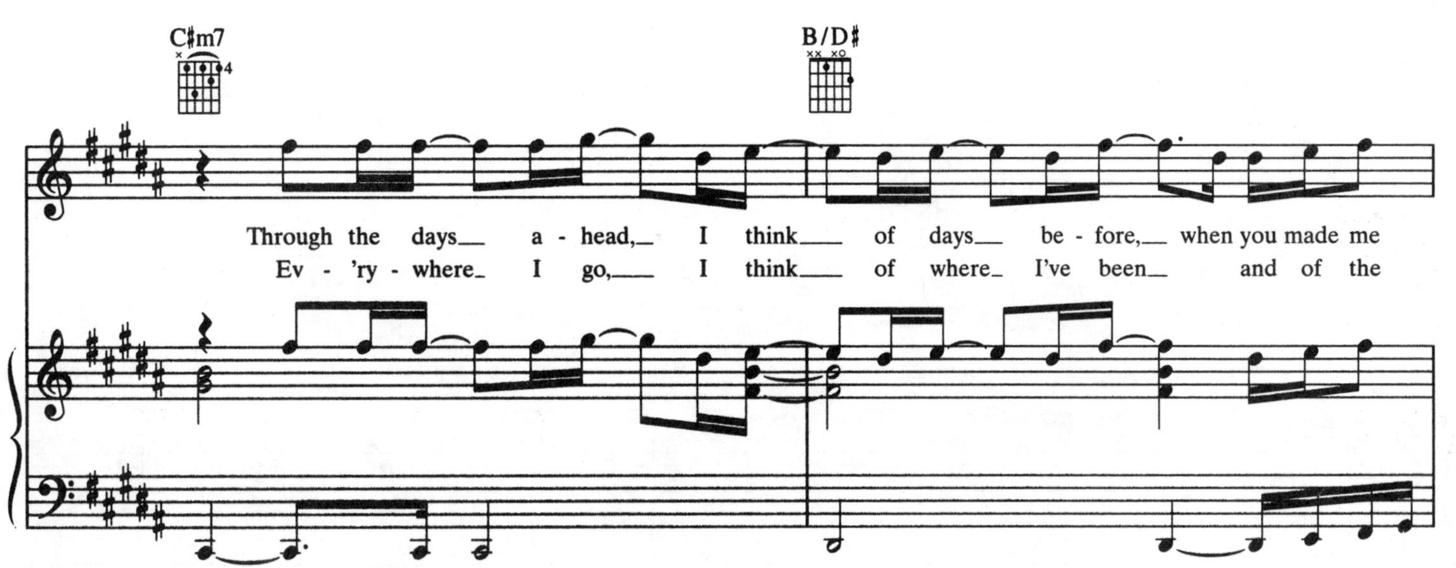

Amaj9
C♯m7/F♯
hope for some - thing bet - ter and made me reach for some - thing more.
one who knew me bet - ter than an - y - one ev - er will a - gain.
You taught me to run,
Chorus:
B
F♯/A♯
C♯m7
you taught me to fly, helped me to free the me in - side. Helped me hear the
E
B/D♯
C♯m7
C♯m7/F♯
mu - sic of my heart. Helped me hear the mu - sic of my heart. You o-pened my
B
F♯/A♯
Amaj9
eyes, you o-pened the door to some-thing I've nev - er known be - fore. And your

1.
C♯m7
C♯m7/F♯
A2
love is the mu - sic of my heart.
2.
Bridge:
C♯m7
C♯m7/F♯
E
F♯
love is the mu - sic of my heart. What you taught me, on - ly
E/G♯
F♯/A♯
B
your love could ev - er teach me. You got through where no one could reach me be - fore.
(Be -
E
C♯m7
fore.)
Coz you al - ways saw in me all the best

B/D♯
Amaj9
C♯m7/F♯
that I could be.
It was you who set me free. You taught me to run,
B
F♯/A♯
C♯m7
you taught me to fly, helped me to free the me in - side.
Helped me hear the
E
B/D♯
C♯m7
B/D♯
C♯m7/F♯
E♭m7/A♭
mu - sic of my heart. Helped me hear the mu - sic of my heart. You taught me to run,
Chorus:
D♭
A♭/C
E♭m7
you taught me to fly, helped me to free the me in - side. Helped me hear the

G♭
D♭/F
E♭m7
D♭
A♭/C
E♭m7/A♭
music of my heart. Helped me hear the music of my heart. You opened my
D♭
A♭/C
C♭maj9
eyes, you opened the door to something I've never known before. And your
E♭m7
E♭m7/A♭
C♭2
love is the music of my heart,
rit.
D♭
is the music of my heart.

WHEN I SAID I DO

Words and Music by
CLINT BLACK

When I Said I Do - 4 - 1

A
B♭
E
F
We take 'em all the way that we should.__ To -
D
E♭
geth - er, you and me,__ for - sak - ing them all.__
F♯m
Gm
E
F
Deep in the night and by the light__ of day,__ it
D
E♭
al - ways looks the same.__ True love al - ways does.__
A
B♭
E/G♯
F/A
And here by your side,__ we're a mil - lion miles a - way.__ Noth - ing's

D
E♭
ev - er gon - na change the way I feel. The way it is is the way that it
Chorus:
A B♭
E F
Bm7 Cm7
was. When I said I do, I meant that I will,
D E♭
Bm7/E Cm7/F
A B♭
'til the end of all time, be faith - ful and
E F
G A♭
D E♭
true, de - vot - ed to you. That's what I had in mind when
1.
A B♭
D/A E♭/B♭
I said I do.
2. Well, this

Verse 2:
Well, this old world keeps changin'
And the world stays the same
For all who came before.
And it goes hand in hand,
Only you and I can undo
All that we became.
That makes us so much more
Than a woman and a man.
And after everything that comes and goes around
Has only passed us by,
Here alone in our dreams,
I know there's a lonely heart in every lost and found.
But forever you and I will be the ones
Who found out what forever means.
(To Chorus:)

YOUR LOVE AMAZES ME

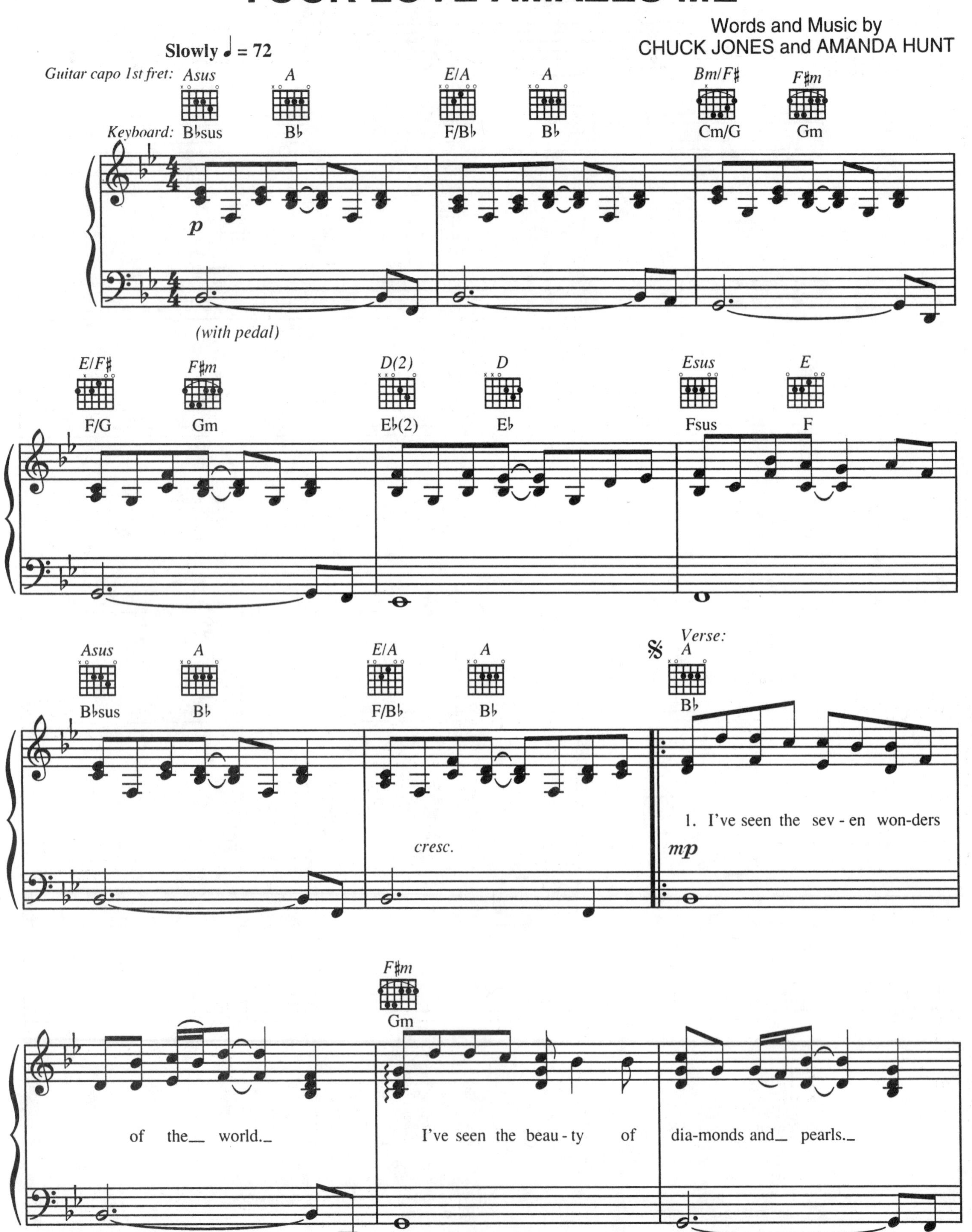

D
E♭
Esus
Fsus
E
F
1.
Asus
B♭sus
A
B♭
But they ain't noth-in', ba - by,
your love a - maz - es me.
E/A
F/B♭
A
B♭
2.
Asus
B♭sus
A
B♭
To next strain
E/A
F/B♭
A
B♭
cresc.
3.
Asus
B♭sus
A
B♭
cresc.
Chorus:
C♯m
Dm
D
E♭
mf
Don't you ev - er doubt this
love of mine.
A
B♭
Esus
Fsus
E
F
You're the on - ly one for me.

Bm
Cm
F♯m
Gm
You give me hope, you give_ me rea - son.
You give me some - thing_ to be - lieve_ in.
G
A♭
Esus
Fsus
E
F
For - ev - er faith - ful - ly,___
you love a - maz - es me.__
Asus
B♭sus
A
B♭
E/A
F/B♭
1.
mp
dim.
D.S. 𝄋
2.
Bm/F♯
Cm/G
F♯m
Gm
E/F♯
F/G
Your love,___

Verse 2:
I've seen a sunset that would make you cry,
And colors of a rainbow reaching 'cross the sky.
The moon in all its phases, but
Your love amazes me.
To Chorus:

Verse 3:
I've prayed for miracles that never came.
I got down on my knees in the pouring rain.
But only you could save me,
Your love amazes me.
(To Chorus:)

MY ONE TRUE FRIEND
(from "ONE TRUE THING")

Words and Music by
CAROLE BAYER SAGER, CAROLE KING
and DAVID FOSTER

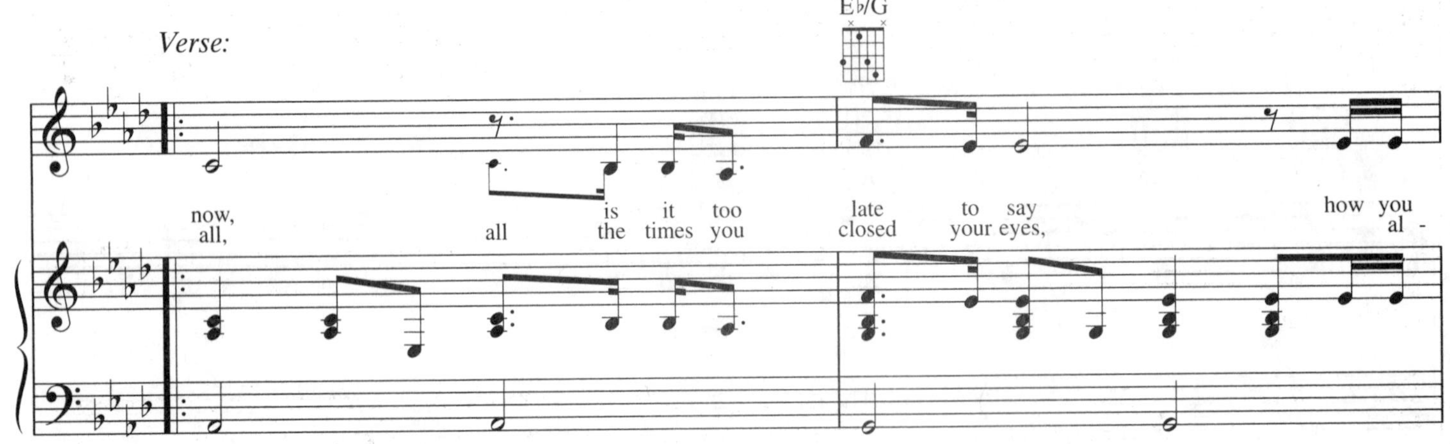

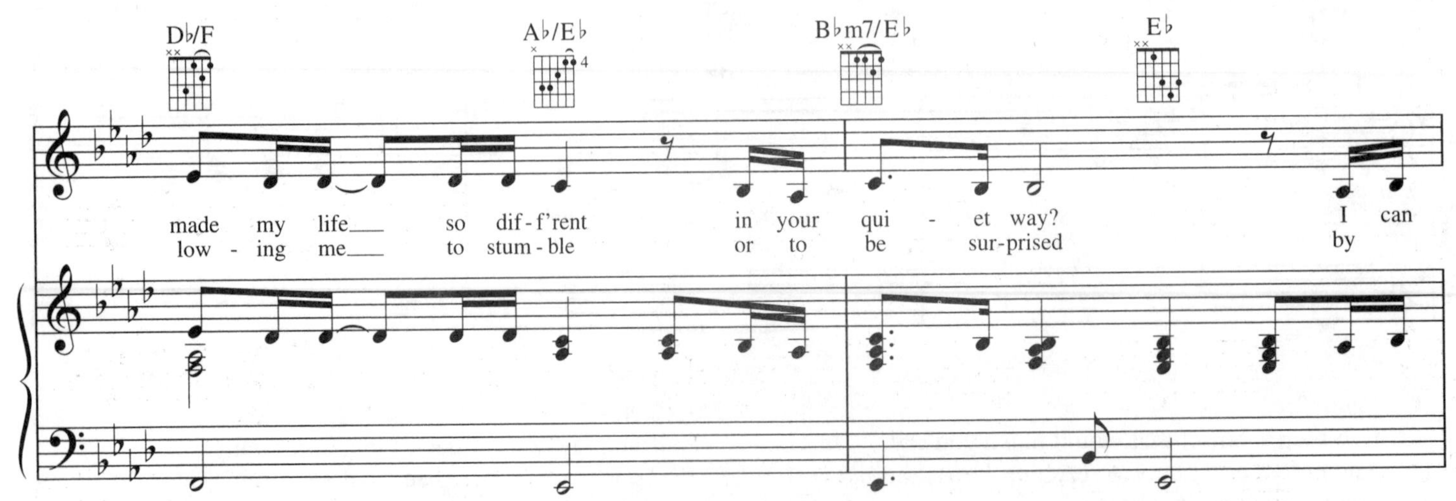

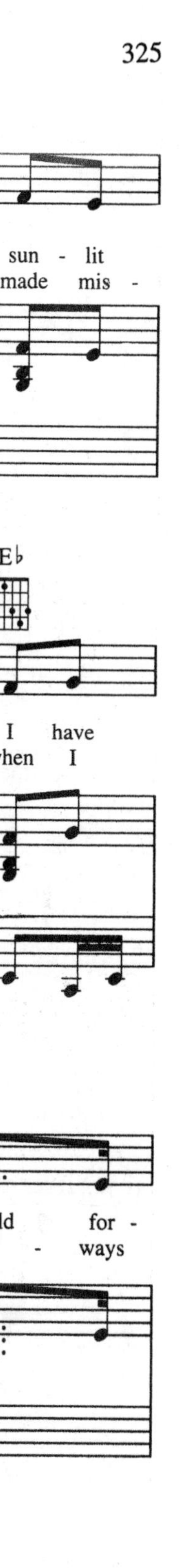
A♭
E♭/G
see the joy in simple things; a sunlit
life with all its twists and turns. I've made mis-
D♭/F
A♭/E♭
B♭m7/E♭
E♭
B♭m7/E♭
E♭
sky and all the songs we used to sing. I have
takes; you always knew that I would learn. And when I
Fm
A♭/E♭
D♭
walked and I have prayed I could for-
left, it's you who stayed. You always
A♭/E♭
C7/E
Fm
A♭/E♭
give and we could start again. In the
knew that I'd come home again. In the

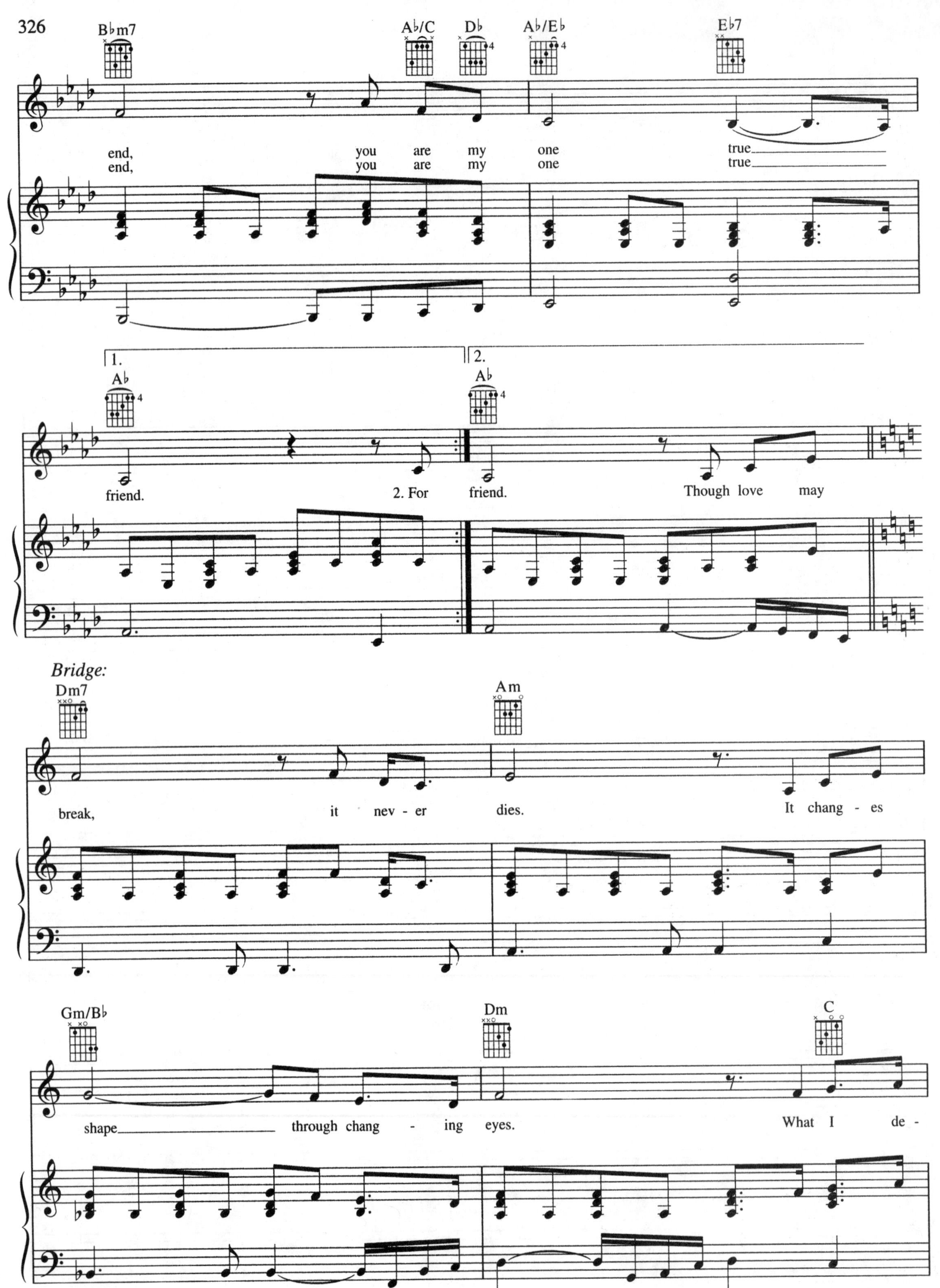
B♭m7
A♭/C
D♭
A♭/E♭
E♭7
end, you are my one true
end, you are my one true
1.
A♭
2.
A♭
friend. 2. For friend. Though love may
Bridge:
Dm7
Am
break, it nev - er dies. It chang - es
Gm/B♭
Dm
C
shape through chang - ing eyes. What I de -

F
Em
nied I now can see. You al - ways
Dm
C/G
G
Fmaj7/G
G
were the light in - side of me.
A
E/G♯
I know, I know, I know, I know it was you.
D/F♯
A/E
E
I have

F♯m A/E D A/E C♯7/E♯

walked and I have prayed I could for - give and we could start a -

F♯m A/E Bm7 A/C♯ D

gain. In the end, you are my

A/E E7 A Dmaj7 D6 A Dmaj9 Bm7/E

one true friend, my one true friend. I al - ways, al - ways

A Dmaj9 D6 A Dmaj9 D6 A

knew, I al - ways knew that it was you, my one true friend.

rit.

SOMETHING THAT WE DO

Guitar originally recorded in alternate tuning (open D) w/capo at 5th fret:
⑥ = D ③ = F♯
⑤ = A ② = A
④ = D ① = D

Words and Music by
CLINT BLACK and SKIP EWING

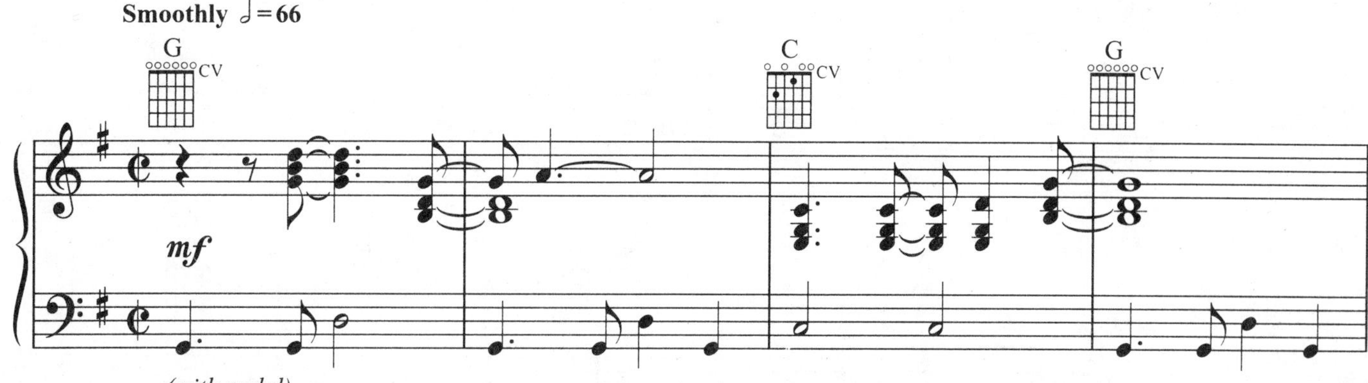

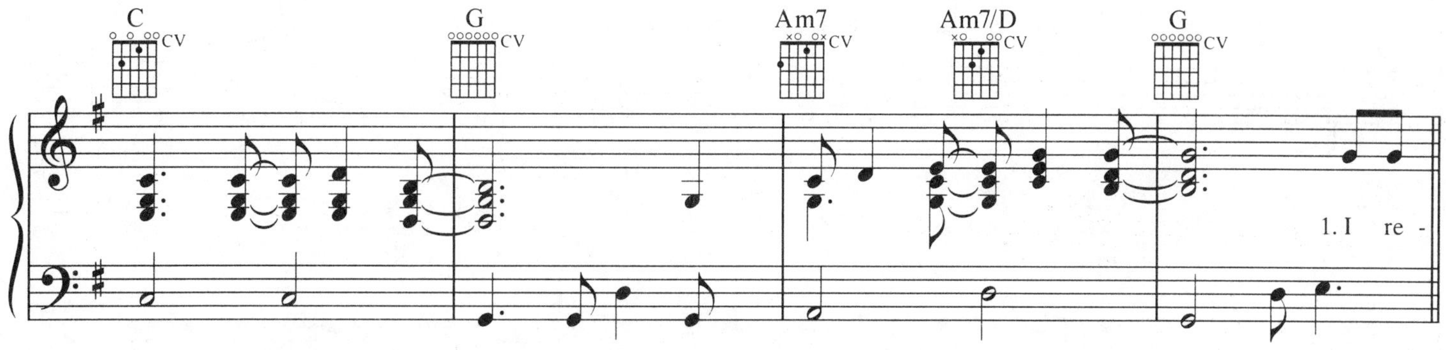

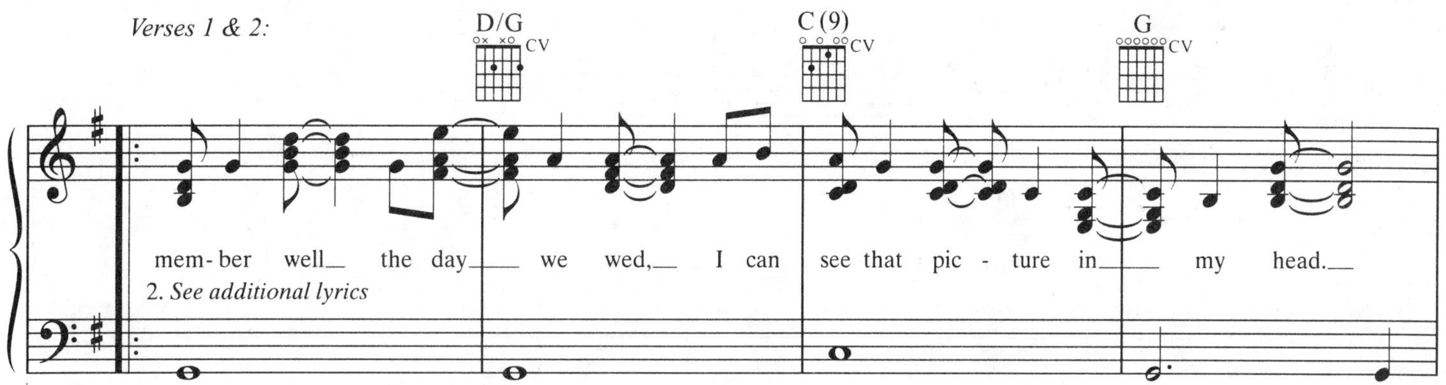

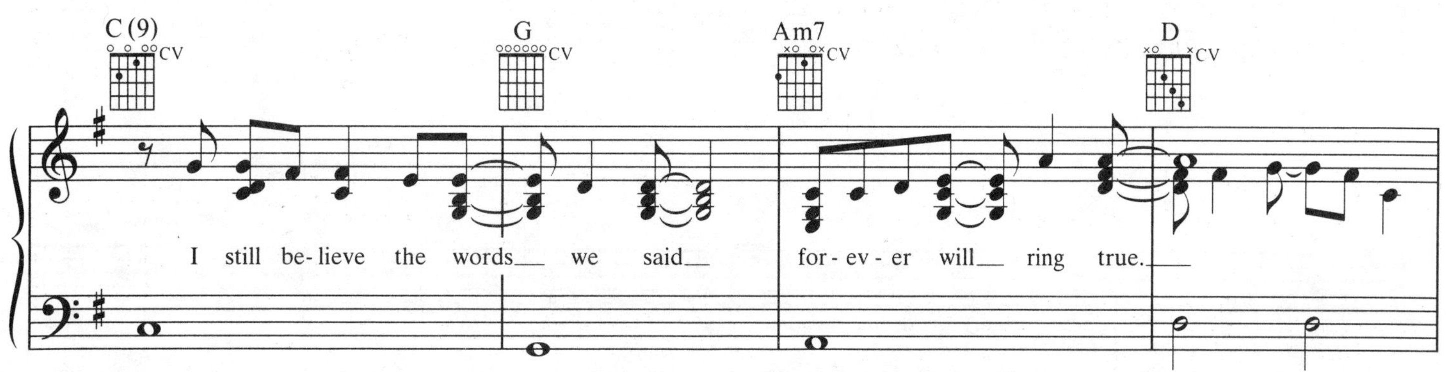

G
D/G
C
G
Love is cer - tain, love is kind, love is yours_ and love is mine._ But it
C
G
Am7
D7sus
1.
G
is - n't some - thing that__ we find, it's some-thing that__ we do.__ 2. It's
2.
G
% Bridge:
C
G/B
We help_ to make_ each oth - er all__ that we_ can__
Am7
G
be,__ though we can find our strength and in - spi - ra - tion in - de - pend - ent - ly._
C
G/B
The way we work_ to - geth - er is__ what sets__ our love_ a - part,

B♭
To Coda
Am7
so close - ly that we can't tell where I
end and where you
rit.
D
Verse 3:
G
D/G
C(9)
start. 3. It
gives me heart, re - mem - b'ring how we start - ed with a sim -
a tempo
G
C(9)
G
Am7
ple vow. There's so much to look back on now.
Still it feels brand new.
D
G
D/G
C
We're on a road that has no end, and each day we be - gin
G
C
G
Am7
D7sus
a - gain. Love's not just some - thing that we're in, it's some - thing that we do.

G
CV
D/G
C
G
D.S. 𝄋 al Coda
C
G
Am7
D7sus
G
G/B
Coda
Am7
D
G
end and where you start.
rit.
Love is wide,
a tempo
D/G
C/G
G
C/G
love is long, love is deep and love is strong.
Love is why I love
G
Am7
D
G
this song, I hope you love it, too.
I re - mem-ber well the day

Verse 2:
It's holding tight, lettin' go,
It's flyin' high and layin' low.
Let your strongest feelings show
And your weakness, too.
It's a little and a lot to ask,
An endless and a welcome task.
Love isn't something that we have,
It's something that we do.
(To Bridge:)

NOW AND FOREVER

Words and Music by
RICHARD MARX

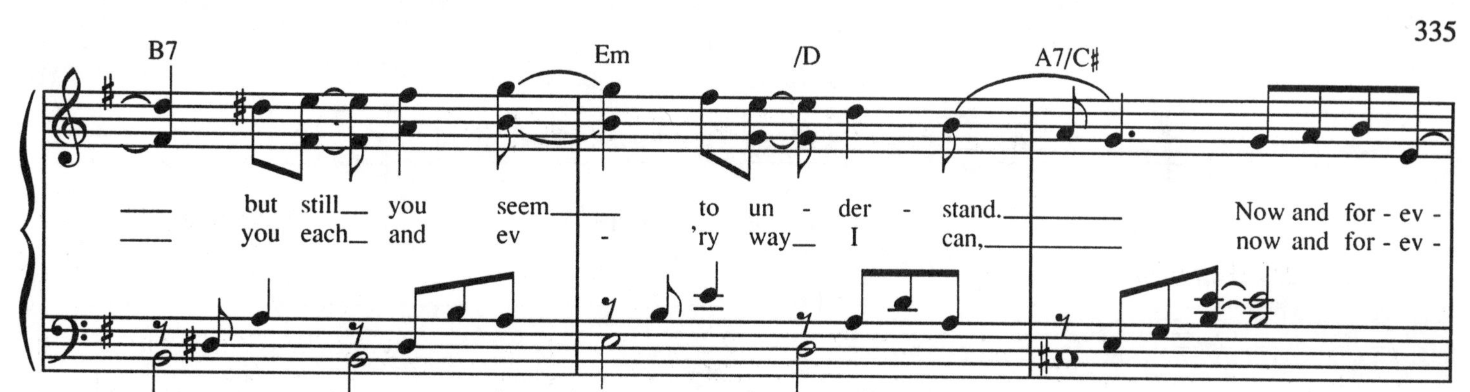
B7
Em
/D
A7/C♯
but still__ you seem__ to un - der - stand.__ Now and for - ev -
you each__ and ev - 'ry way__ I can,__ now and for - ev -

Am7
C/D
D
1.
G
C/G
- er,__ I will be__ your man.__
- er,__ I will be__ your man.__

2.
G
C/G
B7
Bridge:
Em
C
Now I can rest__ my wor - ries and
mf

G
D
Em
C
G
D/F♯
al - ways be sure__ that I won't__ be a - lone__ an - y - more.__

Em C G D Am7
If I'd on-ly known you were there all the time, all this time.
Cm(♯7) Cm6 G D/F♯ Em
3
3
Am Em/G D/F♯ G D/F♯
3
3
Em Am Em/G D/F♯
C B7 Em /D
Un-til the day the o-cean does-n't touch the sand,

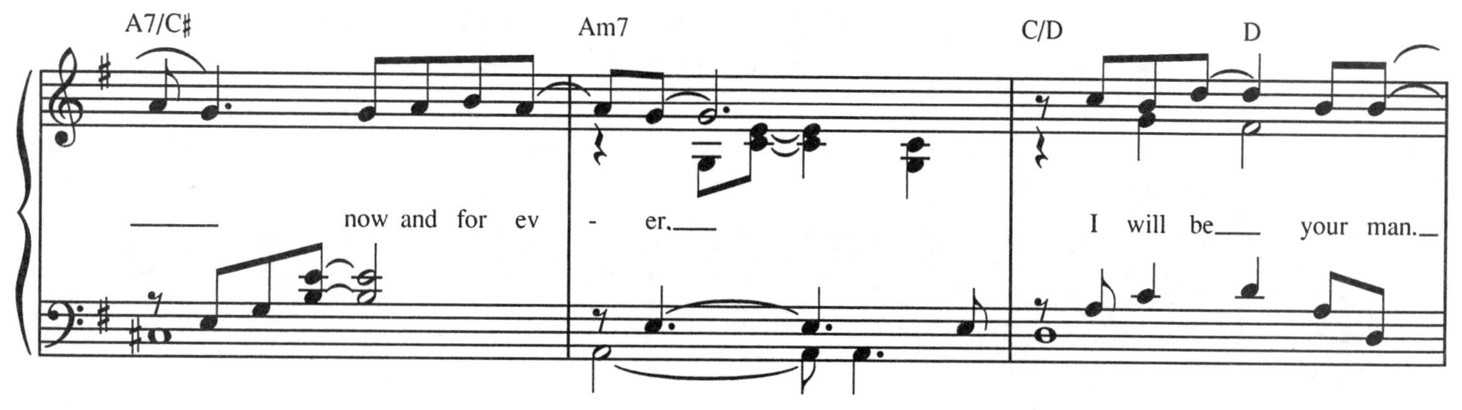
A7/C♯
Am7
C/D
D
now and for ev - er.
I will be your man.

G
C/G
Am7
Now and for - ev - er,

C/D
D
C
I will be your man.

Cm6
G
C/G
D/G
G
poco rit. e dim.
mp

OH HOW THE YEARS GO BY

Words and Music by
WILL JENNINGS and SIMON CLIMIE

Verse:
D(9)
A
E/G♯
1. In our times_ of trou-ble, we on-ly had_ our-selves,
2. See additional lyrics
F♯m
D(9)
no-bod-y else._ No one there to save us,___ we had to save_ our-
A
E/G♯
F♯m
D(9)
selves. And when the storms came_ through,_
E
F♯m
E
_ they found me and you, ooh, back to-geth - er.

D(9)
F♯m
And when the sun would_ shine,___ it was yours and mine, yours and mine for -
𝄋 Chorus:
E
A
Dmaj9
E
ev - er. And, oh, how the years go by.___
A
Dmaj9
E
A
Dmaj9
Oh, how the love brings tears___ to my eyes._ All through the chang - es the
To Coda 𝄌 1.
E
F♯m
A
D(9)
E
soul_ nev-er dies.___ We fight,___ we laugh,_ we cry___ as the years___ go_

A
D(9)
E
D/E
E
by.
2.
E
A
D(9)
E
as the years go by.
(Oh, how the years go by.)
Bridge:
C♯m
E
And if we lose our way
an-y night or day,
C♯m
Bm7
F♯m7
well, we'll al - ways be where we should be. I'm there

D
D/E
D
E/D
for you, and I know you're there for me.
D
A
E/G♯
F♯m
A/E
As the years go by.
D(9)
E/D
D(9)
F♯m
You know you're not a - lone in this world of
D.S. 𝄋 al Coda
A/E
E
Dmaj9
E/G♯
stran - gers. And

Verse 2:
There were times we stumbled,
They thought they had us down,
We came around.
How we rolled and rambled,
We got lost and we got found.
Now we're back on solid ground.
We took everything
All our times would bring
In this world of danger.
'Cause when your heart is strong,
You know you're not alone
In this world of strangers.
(To Chorus:)

SHE'S ALL I EVER HAD

Words and Music by
ROBI ROSA, GEORGE NORIEGA
and JON SECADA

Moderately slow ♩ = 82

B(9)
4

Verse:

1. Here I am,
bro - ken wings.
2. So much time,
so much pain, but

Qui - et thoughts,
un - spo - ken dreams.
there's one thing
that still re - mains.

Here I am, a - lone a - gain.
It's the way she cared, the love we shared.
I need her now to hold my hand. She's
And through it all, she's al - ways been there. She's
Pre-chorus:
G♯m7
F♯
all, she's all I ev - er
all, she's all I ev - er
all, she's all I ev - er
E(9)
F♯
had. She's the air I breathe. She's
had. In a world so cold, so emp - ty, she's
had. I have to make her see, yeah. She's

G♯m7 F♯

all, she's all I ev - er had.
all, she's all I ev - er had.
all, she's all I ev - er had.

E(9) Em6

Chorus:

B F♯/B

It's the way she makes me feel, it's the on - ly thing that's real.

B
F♯/B
And when I look in - to her eyes, it's the way I feel in - side,
E
To Coda
Em6
like the man I want to be. She's all I'll ev - er need.
B(9)
4
1.
2.

D.S. 𝄋 al Coda

She's__

𝄌 *Coda*

Em6 B

__ She's all__ I'll ev - er need.__ It's the way she makes__ me feel,__

__ she's my lov - er, she's__ my friend.__ And when I look in - to__ her eyes,__

F♯/B
E
it's the way I feel in - side,
like the man I want to be.
Em6
B(9)
She's all I'll ev - er need.
Here I am.

SOMETHING ABOUT THE WAY YOU LOOK TONIGHT

Lyrics by
BERNIE TAUPIN

Music by
ELTON JOHN

F#
A#m7
Oh I need to tell__ you how you light up ev - ery sec - ond of the day,__
smile__ you pull the deep - est sec - rets from my heart.
D#m
F#/C#
B
but in the moon - light__ you just
In all hon - est - y__ I'm
G#m7
C#
shine like a bea - con on__ the bay.__
speech - less and I don't know where to start.__
And I can't ex -
F#
A#7
D#m
-plain__ but it's some - thing a - bout__ the way__ you look to - night.

D#7
G#m
G#m7
It takes my breath a - way.
It's that feel - ing I get a - bout you
C#
F#
deep in - side.
And I can't des - cribe
but it's
A#7
D#m
F#/C#
B
F#/A#
G#m
F#
fr 3
some - thing a - bout the way you look to - night.
It takes my breath a - way,
C#
1.
F#
C#
the way you look to - night.
With your

2.
F♯
fr 4 A B F♯
night. The way you look to - night. The way you
fr 4 A B F♯ fr 4 A B F♯
look to - night. The way you look to - night. The way you
fr 4 A B F♯ fr 4 A B F♯ fr 4 A B F♯
look to - night. The way you look to - night. The way you look to - night.
fr 4 A B F♯ fr 4 A B F♯
The way you look to - night. The way you look to - night.

TELL HIM

Words and Music by
LINDA THOMPSON, DAVID FOSTER
and WALTER AFANASIEFF

Slowly ♩ = 76
G♯m
Verse:
Celine:
1. I'm scared,
mp
(with pedal)
D♯m/F♯
so a-fraid to show I care.
Will__ he think me
E
C♯m
B
weak if I trem-ble when I speak?
simile

D♯/F𝄪
G♯m
Ooh, what if there's an - oth - er one_ he's
2. See additional lyrics
mf
D♯m/F♯
Emaj7
F♯/E
think-ing of? May - be he's in love. I'd feel like a
D♯m7
G♯m7
C♯m7
B
fool. Life can be so cruel. I don't know what to do.
Emaj7
Barbra:
I've been there, with my heart_ out in my

D♯m7
G♯m7
D
hand.
But what you must un - der - stand,
you can't let the
A/C♯
E
chance to love him pass you by.
Chorus:
A
F♯m7
Both:
Tell him, tell him that the sun and moon rise
D6
Bm7(♭5)/E
E
A
in his eyes. Reach out to him and whis - per

F♯m7
Dmaj7
Celine:
ten - der words so soft and sweet. I'll hold him close to feel his heart beat.
1.
Bm7/E
E
A
Barbra:
Love will be the gift you give your - self.
2.
Bm7/E
A
Celine:
Love will be the gift you give your - self.
Bridge:
F
B♭maj7
Em7
C/E
Dm7
G7/B
Love is light that sure - ly glows in the hearts of those who know. It's a stead - y flame that

C
A♭
D♭maj7
Cm7
Fm7
Barbra:
Celine:
grows. Feed the fire with all the pas-sion you can show. To-night,
B♭m7
A♭/C
D♭maj7
E♭/F
Fm7
Barbra:
love will as-sume it's place. This mem-'ry time can-not e-rase.
B♭m7
A♭/C
Fsus
F
Both:
Your faith will lead love where it has to go.
rall.
B♭
Gm7
E♭6
Tell him, tell him that the sun and moon rise in his eyes. Reach
a tempo

Verse 2:
(Barbra:)
Touch him with the gentleness you feel inside. (*C:* I feel it.)
Your love can't be denied.
The truth will set you free.
You'll have what's meant to be.
All in time, you'll see.
(Celine:)
I love him, *(B:* Then show him.*)*
Of that much I can be sure. *(B:* Hold him close to you.)
I don't think I could endure
If I let him walk away
When I have so much to say.
(To Chorus:)

TO LOVE YOU MORE

Words and Music by
JUNIOR MILES and DAVID FOSTER

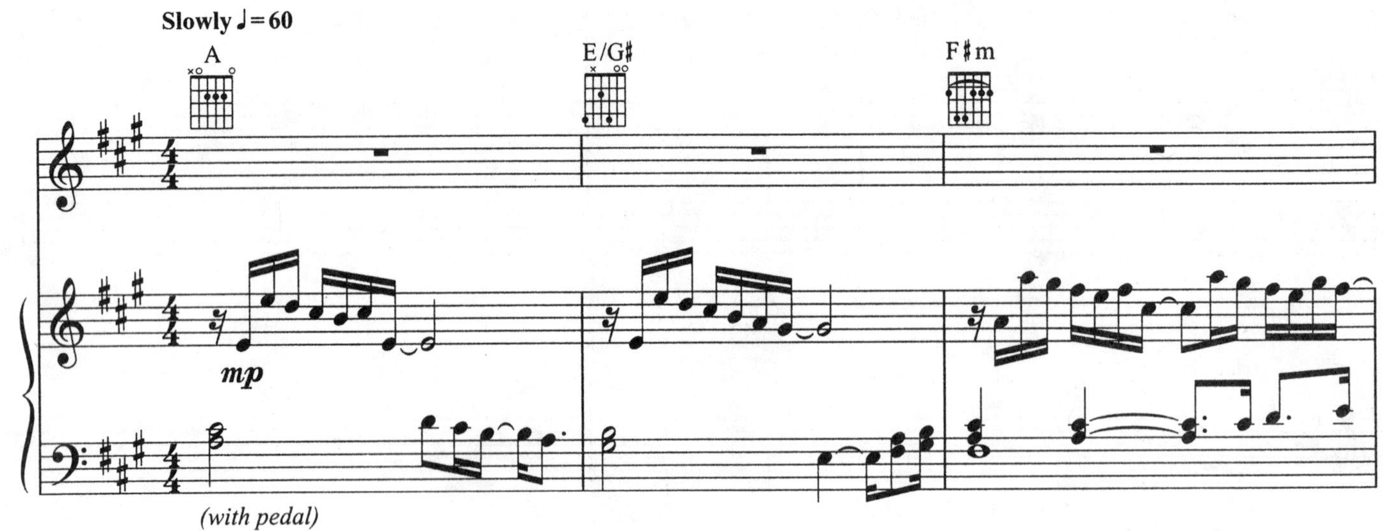

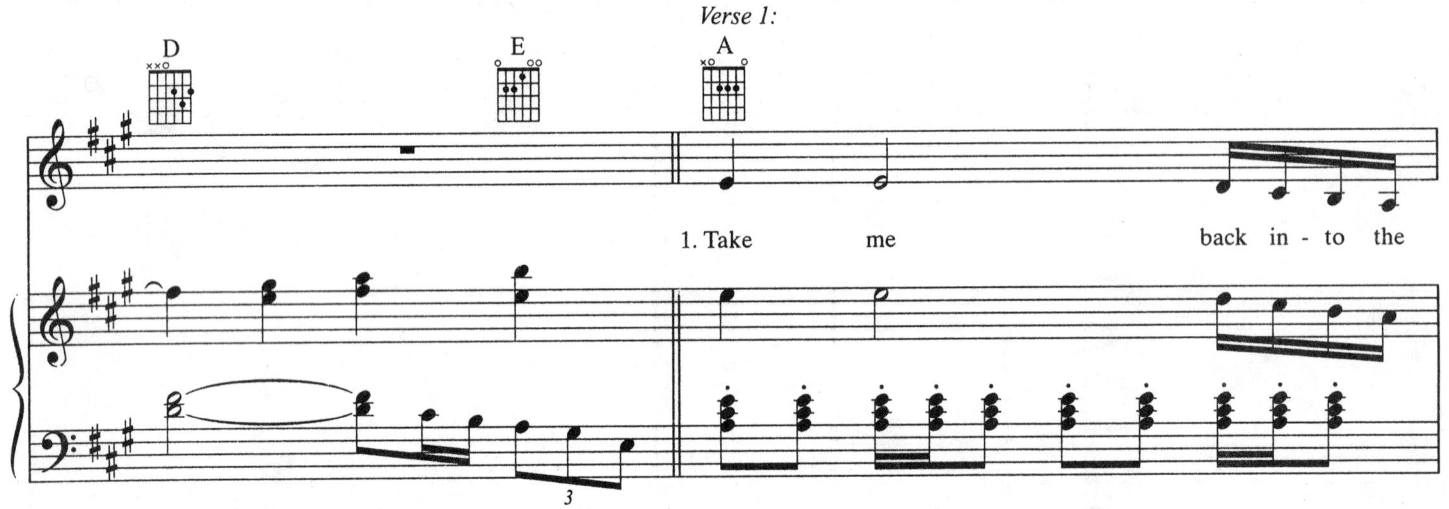

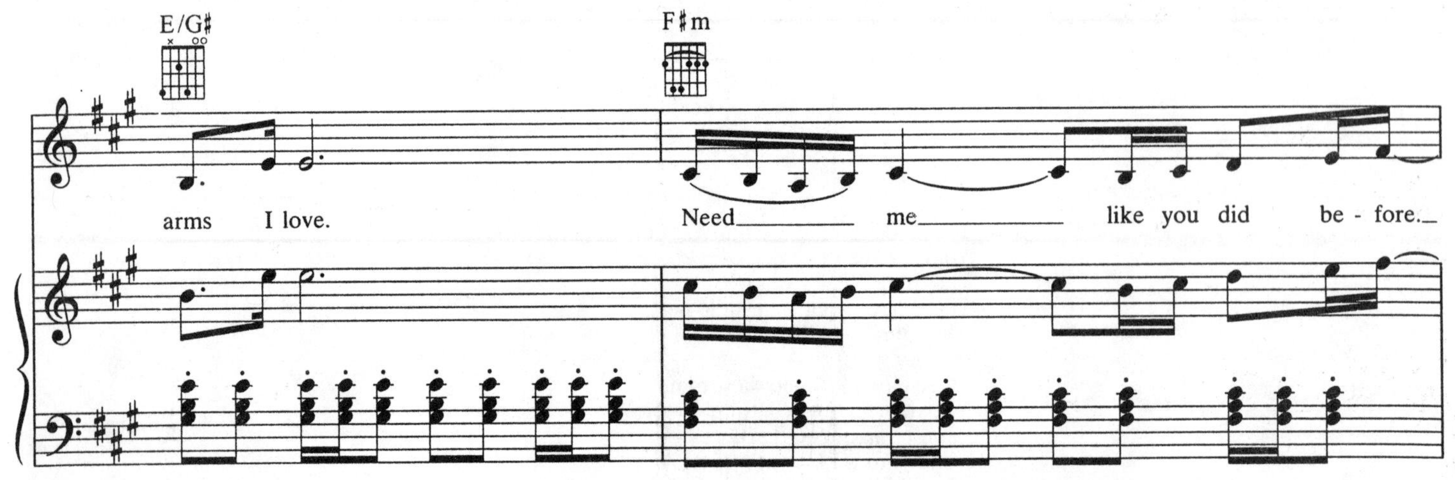

D
E/D
A/C♯
Am/C
Touch me once a-gain and re-
G/B
Gm/B♭
Dm/A
A
mem-ber when there was no one that you want-ed
E7sus
Verses 2 & 3:
A
more.
2. Don't go, you know you will
3. See me as if you
cresc.
mf
E
F♯m
break my heart. She won't love you like I
nev-er knew. Hold me so you can't let

D
E/D
A/C♯
Am/C
will.
I'm the one who'll stay
when she
go.
Just be - lieve in me,
I will
G/B
Gm/B♭
Dm
A
walks a - way,
and you know
I'll be stand - ing here still.
make you see
all the things
that your heart needs to know.
Esus
E
Chorus:
A
E
I'll be wait - ing for you,
F♯m
C♯m
D
A/E
E
here in - side my heart.
I'm the one
who wants to love you more.

A
E7sus
E7
A
E
You will see I can give you
F♯m
C♯m
D
A/E
E
ev-'ry-thing you need. Let me be the one to love you more.
1. A
2. A
And
Bridge 1:
F
Dm
A
some way, all the love that we had can be saved.

F
Dm
Esus
E
Whatever it takes, we'll find a way.
A
B/A
E/G♯
Em/G
D/F♯
C/E
G/D
Am/C
F/A
E/G♯
Be -
Bridge 2:
A
Am
G
Gm
lieve in me, I will make you see all the things
mp

Dm
A
E
Esus
N.C.
that your heart needs to know.
I'll be
cresc.
mf
Chorus:
A
E
F♯m
C♯m
wait - ing for you,
here in - side my heart.
I'm the one
D
A/E
E
A
E7sus
E7
who wants to love you more.
Can't you
A
E
F♯m
C♯m
see I can give you
ev - 'ry - thing you need?
Let me be

D
A/E
E
A
the one to love you more.
A
E
F♯m
C♯m
Oh.
D
A/E
E
1.2.3.
A
E7sus
E7
4.
A
A/D
D6
A

UN-BREAK MY HEART

Words and Music by
DIANE WARREN

Bm
Em7
A
F#7
Come back and bring back my smile, come and take these tears a - way. I
Don't leave me here with these tears, come and kiss this pain a - way. I
Bm
Em7
A
need your arms to hold me now. Nights are so un - kind.
can't for - get the day you left. Time is so un - kind,
Bm
Em7
A
A7
Bring back those nights when I held you be - side me.
and life is so cruel with - out you here be - side me.
Un - break my heart,
Chorus:
Dm
Gm7
C
A7
say you love me a - gain. Un - do this hurt

Dm
Gm7
C
A7
_ you caused_ when you walked_ out the door_ and walked out_ of my life._ Un - cry_ these tears_
To Coda
Dm
Gm7
C
A7
_ I cried so man - y nights._ Un - break_ my heart._
1.
2.
C/B♭
B♭
A7
F♯7
D♯
G♯m
C♯m7
F♯
D♯m7

G♯m
C♯m7
F♯7
Bridge:
Bm
Em7
A
Don't leave me in all this pain,
don't leave me out in the rain.
Bm
Em7
A
D.S. 𝄋 al Coda
Bring back those nights when I held you be - side me.
Un - break my heart,
Coda
C
A7
Dm
Gm7
Un - break my, un - break my heart, sweet ba - by.

C
A7
Dm
Gm7
Come back and say you love me.
Un - break my heart, sweet dar - ling.
With - out you, I just can't go on.
Repeat ad lib. and fade

VALENTINE

Composed by
JIM BRICKMAN and JACK KUGELL

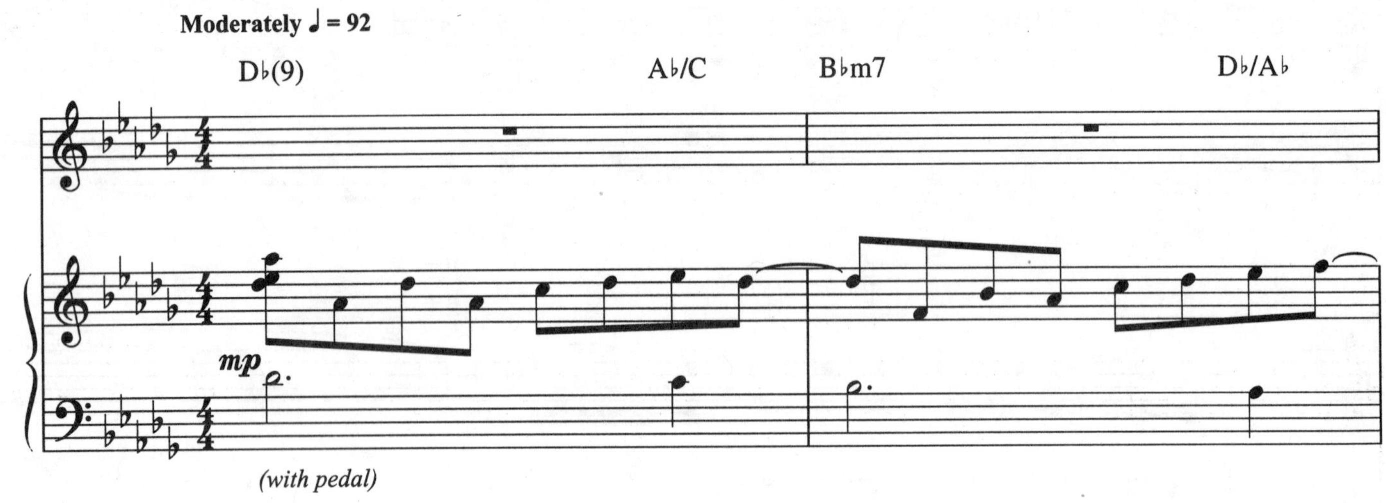

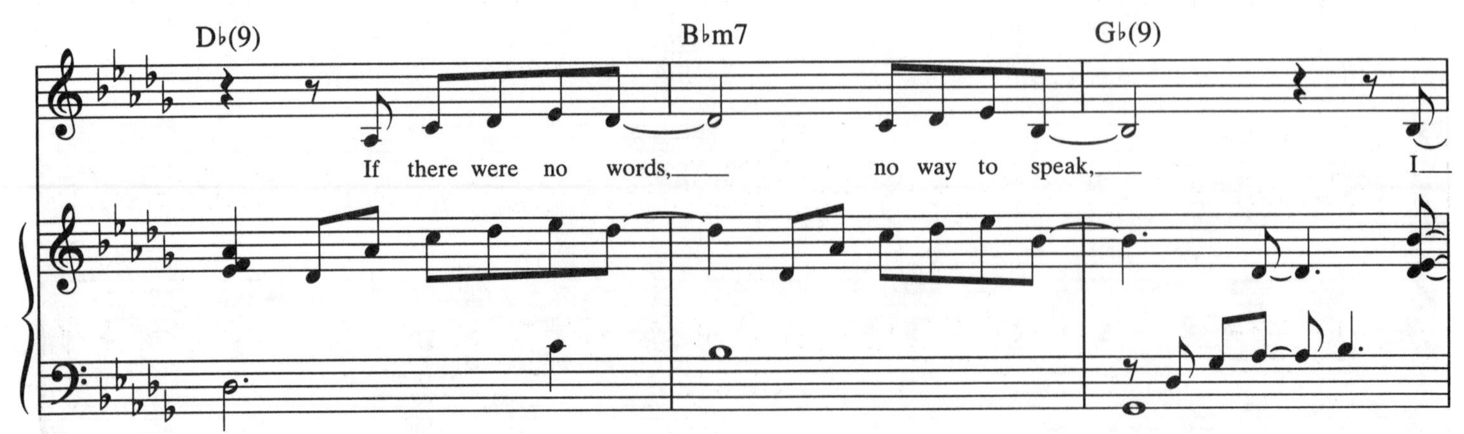

A♭sus
A♭
D♭(9)
B♭m7
would still hear you. If there were no tears, no way to feel
G♭(9)
A♭7sus
D♭(9)/F
inside, I'd still feel for you. And even if the sun
G♭(9)
A♭
Fm7
D♭(9)/F
G♭(9)
A♭
refused to shine, even if romance ran out of rhyme,
E♭m7
F7sus
F7
B♭m
D♭/A♭
you would still have my heart until the end of time.

Gm7(♭5)
D♭/A♭
G♭/A♭
You're all I need, my love, my Val - en - tine.
D♭(9)
A♭/C
B♭m7
D♭/A♭
G♭(9)
G♭/A♭
D♭(9)
B♭m7
G♭(9)
All of my life, I have been wait - ing for all
A♭sus
A♭
D♭(9)
B♭m7
you give to me. You've o - pened my eyes and shown me how

G♭(9)
A♭7sus
A♭
D♭(9)/F
to love unself - ish - ly. I've dreamed of this a thou-
mf
G♭(9)
A♭
Fm7
D♭(9)/F
G♭(9)
A♭
- sand times be - fore, but in my dreams I could - n't love you more.
E♭m7
F7sus
F7
B♭m
D♭/A♭
I will give you my heart un - til the end of time.
Gm7(♭5)
D♭/A♭
G♭/A♭
You're all I need, my love, my Val - en - tine.

D♭(9)
B♭m7
G♭(9)
G♭/B♭
A♭/C
D♭(9)
B♭m7
G♭(9)
D♭/A♭
A♭
And
D♭(9)/F
G♭(9)
A♭
Fm7
D♭(9)/F
e - ven if the sun re - fused to shine, e - ven if ro - mance
G♭(9)
A♭
E♭m7
F7sus
F7
ran out of rhyme, you would still have my heart un - til

B♭m
D♭/A♭
Gm7(♭5)
D♭/A♭
the end of time.
'Cause all I need is you,
G♭/A♭
E♭m7
D♭/F
G♭
my Val - en - tine.
You're
mp
D♭/A♭
G♭/A♭
D♭(9)
A♭/C
all I need, my love, my Val - en - tine.
B♭m7
D♭/A♭
G♭(9)
G♭/A♭
D♭(9)
rit. e dim.
p

THE WAY SHE LOVES ME

Music and Lyrics by
RICHARD MARX

Db
Verse:
1. I'll have this feel - ing 'till the
2. Came close to let - ting this
3. (Instrumental solo ad lib....
day that I die,
train pass me by,
Cb
when I hear my ba - by call - in'.
just like a fool sec - ond guess - in'.
Db
A sim - ple mo - tion, a look in her eyes
I could have spent my life won - der - ing why
Cb
and I'm help - less - ly fall - in'.
I did - n't cher - ish the bless - ing.
...end solo)
Ebm7
I'd give all of
If I'd have known she'd
No - bod - y else could
Ab
some - bod - y else
come my way
do me so right,

D♭
G♭
for any - y piece of her heart that's left.
the lone - ly nights would - 've been o - kay.
a breath of heav - en in my dark - est night.
E♭m7
A♭sus
A♭
She knows me bet - ter than I know my - self.
I have her prom - ise that she's gon - na stay.
I'm gon - na hold on with all of my might.
Chorus:
E
Let me tell you 'bout the way she loves me. Ooh,
F♯m7
I want the world to know.
E
I'm cra - zy 'bout the way she loves me. Ooh,
F♯m7
I'm proud to let it show.
1. 2.
D.S. 𝄋
3.
Repeat ad lib. and fade

YEARS FROM HERE

Words and Music by
GARY BAKER, JERRY WILLIAMS
and FRANK J. MYERS

Bm7
E/G♯
A
D
A/C♯
I don't___ need___
I know___
a crys - tal ball,___
we've just be - gun___
Bm7
E/G♯
D/F♯
E
through your eyes___
and the best___ is
cresc.
I see it all.___
still yet to come.___
Chorus:
A
C♯m7
D
Esus
E
Years from here,___ we'll
mf
look back and treas - ure this
A
F♯m7
D
E
mo - ment for - ev - er in - side___ our hearts.___ And from here___

A
C♯m7
D
C♯
F♯m
A/E
to there, we'll make a mil - lion mem - o - ries that we can share
D
E
To Coda
1. A
A/C♯
D
E7
years from here. dim.
2. D(9)
D.S. % al Coda
D
A/C♯
Bm7
E
dim.
cresc.
Coda
D(9)
dim.
mp
Years from here.
A
A/C♯
D
E7
A
rit. e dim.
p

YOU'RE STILL THE ONE

Words and Music by
SHANIA TWAIN and R.J. LANGE

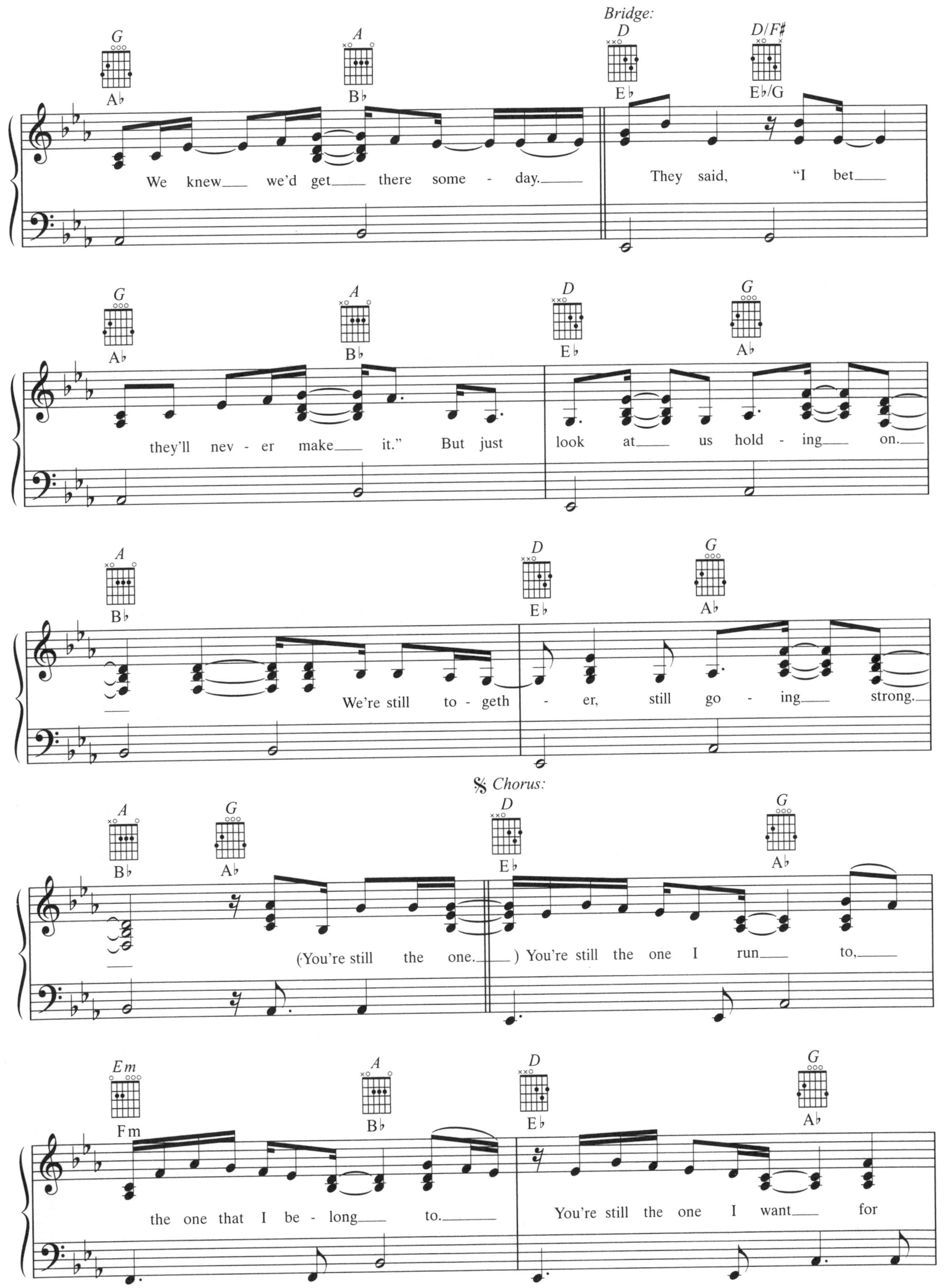
Bridge:
G
A♭
A
B♭
D
E♭
D/F♯
E♭/G
We knew we'd get there some - day.
They said, "I bet
they'll nev - er make it." But just
look at us hold - ing on.
We're still to - geth - er, still go - ing strong.
Chorus:
Em
Fm
(You're still the one.) You're still the one I run to,
the one that I be - long to.
You're still the one I want for

Verse 2:
Ain't nothin' better,
We beat the odds together.
I'm glad we didn't listen.
Look at what we would be missin'
(To Bridge:)

LOVE IS A GIFT

Words and Music by OLIVIA NEWTON-JOHN,
VICTORIA SHAW and EARL ROSE

Gm7
C7sus
C7
B♭/F
F
All at once, I make sense of this crazy world.
B♭/F
C
F
Loved you for so long.
B♭
Gm7
Now your hand is holding mine. It's like we're standing
Chorus:
B♭/C
C7
C7sus
C7
F
B♭
still in time. This is our moment,
cresc.
mf

C F C/E Dm B♭ Gm7 C7sus C7

this is our night. A new be-gin - ning of the rest of our lives.

F B♭ C Dm

With ev - 'ry heart-beat, with ev - 'ry kiss, let's

B♭2 C7sus 1. F/A B♭(9)

al - ways re - mem - ber that love is a gift.

Gm7 C7sus 2. F *Bridge:* Gm7 F/A

a gift. The rar - est thing we have on earth

dim. *cresc.* *f*

B♭ F/A Gm7 F/A B♭(9) C
is so spe - cial, there's no mea - sur - ing its worth.
rit.

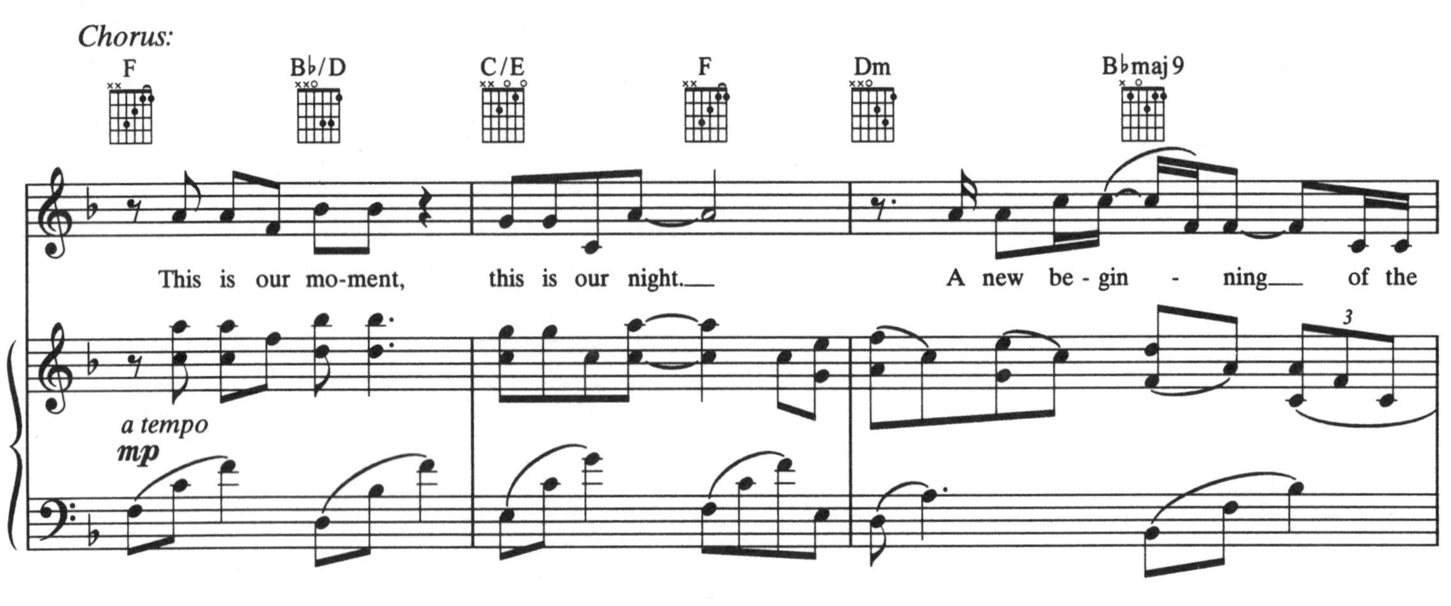
Chorus:
F B♭/D C/E F Dm B♭maj9
This is our mo-ment, this is our night.
A new be - gin - ning of the
a tempo
mp

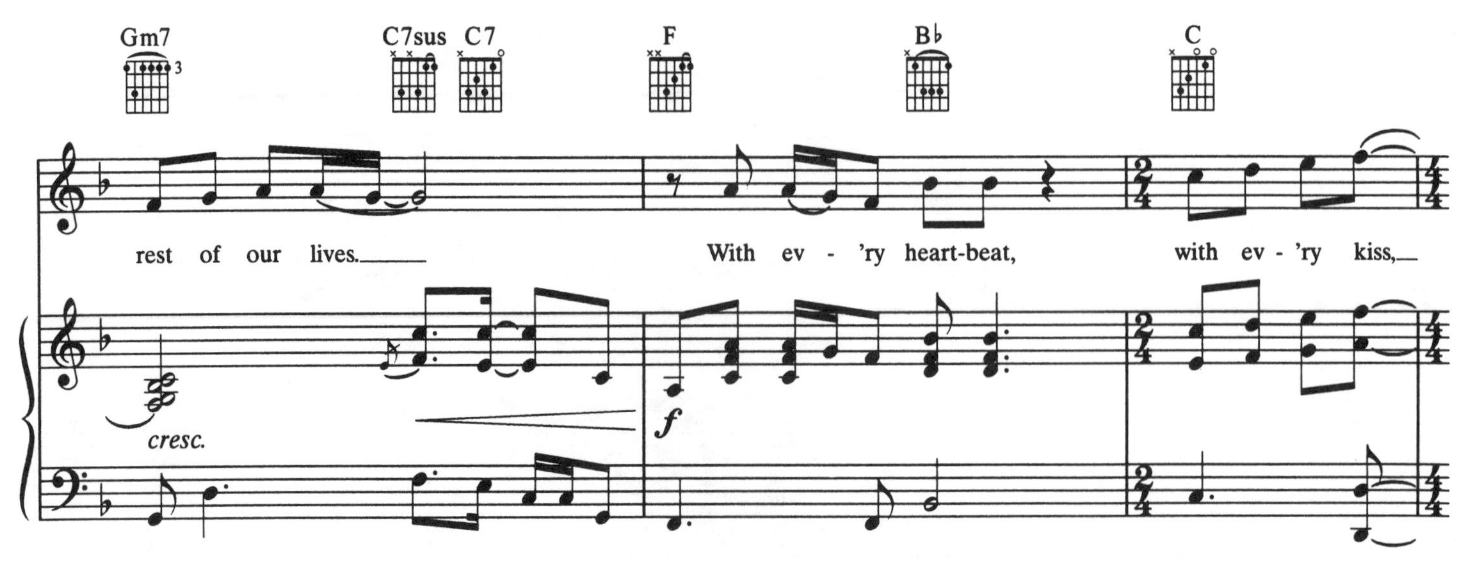
Gm7 C7sus C7 F B♭ C
rest of our lives.
With ev - 'ry heart-beat, with ev - 'ry kiss,
cresc.
f

Verse 2:
With each passing year
We will keep our love alive.
I will be here by your side
Forever.
Looking in your eyes,
I believe in destiny,
I believe in you and me.
(To Chorus:)

TEN YEARS OF MUSIC HISTORY
REMEMBERING THE '90s SERIES

This series is an anthology of music from 1990-2000. Each volume includes artists' works and biographies!

Ten Years of Pop Music History
The Red Book

(MFM0004)

Titles include: All for Love • Always Be My Baby • ...Baby One More Time • Believe • Coming Out of the Dark • Foolish Games • Here I Am (Come and Take Me) • How 'Bout Us • I Don't Want to Miss a Thing • Just Another Day • (God Must Have Spent) A Little More Time on You • More Than Words • Music of My Heart • Show Me the Way • Smooth • Something to Talk About • That's the Way It Is • Un-Break My Heart • You Were Meant for Me and many more.

Ten Years of Pop Music History
The Blue Book

(MFM0005)

Titles include: Back at One • Because You Loved Me • Breakfast at Tiffany's • Change the World • Constant Craving • Don't Cry for Me Argentina • Dreaming of You • From a Distance • Genie in a Bottle • I Do (Cherish You) • I Will Always Love You • If It Makes You Happy • Ironic • Killing Me Softly • Larger Than Life • Love Is All Around • Love Will Keep Us Alive • One of Us • Sunny Came Home and many more.

Ten Years of Country Music History
The Orange Book

(MFM0006)

Titles include: Angels Among Us • Any Man of Mine • A Bad Goodbye • Don't Take the Girl • Forever's As Far As I'll Go • From Here to Eternity • Go Away, No Wait a Minute • I Can Love You Like That • I Cross My Heart • I Do (Cherish You) • I Swear • I'd Like to Have That One Back • If Tomorrow Never Comes • The River • This Kiss • A Thousand Miles from Nowhere • Unanswered Prayers • When You Say Nothing at All • You Light Up My Life and many more.

Ten Years of Country Music History
The Green Book

(MFM0007)

Titles include: Amazed • Breathe • Commitment • The Dance • From This Moment On • How Do I Live • In Another's Eyes • My Maria • Please Remember Me • Pocket of a Clown • Put Yourself in My Shoes • Something in Red • Standing Outside the Fire • Strawberry Wine • There's Your Trouble • 26¢ • Two Sparrows in a Hurricane • What Might Have Been • Years From Here and many more.

Ten Years of Movie Music History
The Yellow Book

(MFM0009)

Titles include: Against the Wind (from *Forest Gump*) • At the Beginning (from *Anastasia*) • Don't Cry for Me Argentina (from *Evita*) • I Believe I Can Fly (from *Space Jam*) • I Say a Little Prayer (from *My Best Friend's Wedding*) • Music of My Heart (from *Music of the Heart*) • The Prayer (from *Quest for Camelot*) • Take Me to the River (from *The Commitments*) • Theme from *Jurassic Park* • There's Something About Mary (from *There's Something About Mary*) and many more.

Ten Years of Movie Music History
The Purple Book

(MFM0010)

Titles include: Anyone at All (from *You've Got Mail*) • Colors of the Wind (from *Pocahontas*) • Duel of the Fates (from *Star Wars: Episode I The Phantom Menace*) • I Will Remember You (from *The Brothers McMullen*) • Kissing You (Love Theme from *Romeo + Juliet*) • Once in a Lifetime (from *Only You*) • Something to Talk About (from *Something to Talk About*) • That Thing You Do (from *That Thing You Do!*) • Uninvited (from *City of Angels*) and many more.